RHAPSODY LANE

A SELECTION OF WORKS BY
FLOWER CITY WRITERS

Rhapsody Lane

A Selection Of Works By
Flower City Writers

Editors
Rena Flannigan
Konrad Brinck
Bala Menon

TAMARIND TREE BOOKS
Toronto

Tamarind Tree Books Inc.,
14 Ferncastle Crescent,
Brampton, Ontario. L7A 3P2, Canada.

Library and Archives Canada Cataloguing in Publication

Rhapsody Lane: A Selection of Works by Flower City Writers /
Editors, Rena Flannigan, Konrad Brinck, Bala Menon.

Issued in print and electronic formats.
ISBN 978-0-9938199-0-2 (pbk.).--ISBN 978-0-9938199-1-9 (Amazon Kindle)

1. Canadian literature (English)--Ontario--Brampton. 2. Canadian
literature (English)--21st century. I. Flannigan, Rena, editor
II. Brinck, Konrad, editor III. Menon, Bala, editor

PS8233.R48 2014 C810.8'09713535 C2014-905421-1
                                  C2014-905422-X

This book is manufactured under Sustainable Forestry Initiative® (SFI®) Certified Sourcing.

*This book is dedicated to all seniors
who have a story to tell and want
to share it with the world.*

CONTENTS

Contents

Contents

FOREWORD

There is great power in words. We rely on words to define and communicate our relationships to each other and to the world at large. We all tell stories, and are defined by the stories we tell.

We relive our past through stories, sometimes edited by a selective memory. "When did you and grandma first meet?" "What was it like when you lived in Thailand?" Some describe our reactions to things that happen to us such as "You'll never guess what happened to me at the office today" or "You'll be amazed at what I saw at the mall this afternoon."

Although many of our stories involve us, others are re-tellings of accounts of our parents or grandparents, thereby providing a sense of continuity in handing them down. We even tell accounts of things that may have happened to friends or acquaintances. It is through all these stories that other people get to know who we are, what we think and how we feel.

Sometimes, we delve into our imaginations to create stories. We tell them to our children and grandchildren as we put them to bed. We tell them around campfires or to entertain our friends. And although these fictions, which may be inspired by current or historical events, are not about us, they may reveal our feelings, tastes, attitudes and, perhaps, fantasies, through the events and characters portrayed.

Like the artist who exhibits works in a gallery or the performer who appears before a live audience, it takes a lot of courage for the story-teller to become a story-writer and put them into print for all to read.

Rhapsody Lane is a collection of stories and poems by a group of courageous story-writers that make up the Creative Writing Group at the Flower City Recreation Centre.

The authors that make up this group are seniors; most are new-comers to writing and display a lot of talent. From tender love to murder and mayhem, these writers touch on all the emotions whether through creative fiction, memoirs or poetry.

They deal with life's turning points, and on decisions made by or forced upon the protagonists. While there may be occasional flaws in the narrative structure, style or grammar, the feelings portrayed are honest and real, and that is what makes them worth reading.

Although, in the introduction, the word "rhapsody" is defined as an "effusively enthusiastic or ecstatic expression of feeling", I rather like another definition which derives from ancient Greek, i.e., an epic poem, or part of it, of a suitable length for recitation at one time.

Many of the works are complete fiction and encompass a range of genres from the classic "true to life" story to science fiction and fantasy. They focus on relationships - between lovers, spouses, friends and, sometimes, enemies.

Some are quirky, some have a touch of violence and many provide surprise endings. Some are funny; others heart-warming. Some are simple morality tales; others are complex and related to myths and legends. Some tales are dark, and have an other-world-ly, almost *"Twilight Zone"* quality.

A number of the pieces presented are true-life stories, memoirs or family histories. These pieces are not only entertaining in their own right, but represent significant efforts to document events of lives, times and family histories which might otherwise be lost forever.

In the poems found in this anthology, the writers do not hide behind imaginary characters, clever plots or the recollection of past events. These writers use their words to bare their souls and deal directly with their emotions - fond remembrance, loss, and most importantly, hope.

Each contributor to this anthology has something to say, and has discovered an inner desire to write it down and to share it with others, whether it be their feelings, experiences or imaginations. They write with honesty, courage and a freshness of voice. Their words deserve to be read.

TONY VANDER VOET
President, Ontario Society of Artists
November, 2014

INTRODUCTION

In 2007, some members of the Flower City Recreation Centre in Brampton, Ontario, formed a Creative Writing Group.

Rhapsody Lane is a small selection of what has been written over the past several years. A couple of writers, whose works are included here, have passed on to, perhaps, better worlds.

Rhapsody, in its literal sense, means an ecstatic/effusive expression of feeling. In this collection, you will find a wide range of expressions. From short stories to memoirs to creative non-fiction, this volume brings together many voices and experiences from the diverse backgrounds of our authors who found themselves through the Creative Writing Group.

Walking down *Rhapsody Lane* is an exploratory and happy outing. On the way, you will meet salespersons, tour directors, journalists, medical workers, engineers, businesspeople, musicians and others from several countries with fascinating stories to tell. For all of them, *Rhapsody Lane* has no end. There is no destination, the lane itself is the journey of life and it is a one-way street.

This collection spans many genres and generations. You'll find tales from around the corner or from far away places, about love and hate, fear and compassion, friends and foes, brothers and sisters and strangers you might never want to meet.

In the Table of Contents, some of our works are listed as 'stories', although they are not fiction; they are charming or painful memories of a time gone by or a place or a person, remembered for many reasons.

We have, however, called them stories for clarity; they are after all narratives about real or imaginary people and connected events, organized thematically or as part of a storytelling process. The word 'story' is often used as a synonym for 'narrative'; and that is what is meant here. The 'shorts' are just that: pocket stories or what is generally known today as 'flash fiction'.

There are also some poignant poems included.

What ties these works together, however, is the authenticity of their authors and the vivid writing. From this little corner of Canada, maybe all of us can learn some truths about ourselves and gain an awareness of the changing asymmetries in the world around us, as we make our happy way down *Rhapsody Lane*.

It also seemed appropriate to us that the book be dedicated to all those who have stories to tell and strive to share them. Enjoy!

EDITORS
Brampton, November, 2014

JEANETTE CLARKE -I

The Getaway

Click, click, click! Susie's stiletto heels announced one more trip across the shop floor. All male eyes would be on those legs, long and tanned with just a hint of skirt at the top. Susie loved the attention, knew that her dancer's legs were her best feature. She wore her long bleached blonde hair in a centre parting, so that it curtained her face, not her best feature, what with the acne that'd plagued her since she was fourteen.

"Pizza face, pizza face!" her brother taunted. She hated the little runt. Hated the fact that none of the new products that promised smooth skin actually worked. Hated her life in small town U.S.A. and couldn't wait to get out. She needed just $2,000 more.

Susie delivered the new work orders to the supervisor. Since the sawmill, the biggest employer in the small town, had branched out into making furniture, a whole new market had been opened up. During the summer, part-timers had to be brought in and on her way back to the office Susie hoped she'd catch the eye of one of them. She wasn't disappointed.

"Hi, sweet thing," he winked at her. "How 'bout you an' me havin' a drink after work?"

Wayne had a dark and dangerous look.

Susie was all smiles when she got back to her desk. Mr. Jefferson, the boss, was sorting out the pay packets for the part-timers, who got paid in cash every Friday.

"So, what you up to this weekend, Susie, anything exciting?" Mr. Jefferson had asked her that self same question every week for the past eighteen months. Jesus, what a boring man.

She was perched on a stool at the bar, the best place to show off her legs, when Wayne sauntered in, about ten minutes late for their first date.

"So, how long've you lived in this dump?" he asked, his voice soft, full of concern and romance.

"Nineteen years, all my life." Susie answered. "But not for much longer, I'm leaving for the big city soon."

"What you gonna do there?" Wayne asked, swigging a beer.

"Get a job as a dancer. I've always been into dancing; I practice every week at the Rec Centre." Susie's eyes gleamed when she talked about her main interest in life.

"Well, you've certainly got the legs for it." Wayne took another swig of the beer. Pity about the face, he thought, talk about swings and roundabouts.

"We shouldn't be seen in public," Susie told Wayne after a couple of dates, and led him to a secluded meeting place. "It'll keep my mom off my back," she explained.

Her mom said he was a bad lot, and Mr. Jefferson had taken a dislike to him too. "This office is off-limits; keep to the factory side," Mr. Jefferson warned him when he caught Wayne in the office area one afternoon talking to Susie.

Three weeks later, Susie's eyes were bright as she climbed into the pick-up, parked in their secret meeting place.

"So, I'm thinking of movin' on," Wayne announced, anticipating a look of desolation to cloud her spotty face.

"When?" asked Susie, eyes downcast.

"Don't like to be tied down, Susie-Q, so probably in a week or two."

"Take me with you!" she pleaded.

"Now, why would I wanna do that?" He was enjoying himself.

"I've got money; been saving for something special, and I could get a job in the city!"

"And how much would those savings be exactly?" Wayne humoured her.

"Close to a thousand." Susie was proud of her nest egg.

"That wouldn't pay one month's rent in the city. We'd need way more than that." Wayne looked at her expectantly. "I've got a plan," he said.

Somehow, Susie knew he would.

It was late Thursday afternoon, the sawmill and factory quiet. As arranged, Susie would leave the office door unlocked for a few minutes when she went to the washroom. Mr. Jefferson had been to the bank and always counted the payroll before putting it in the safe for Friday's cash paypackets to the part-timers. On Susie's return five minutes later, Mr. Jefferson was lying unconscious on the floor, bound hand and foot and blindfolded.

"Didn't know what hit him!" Wayne grinned as he pushed Susie roughly to the floor and tied her up too.

"See you later," Susie whispered softly into his ear as he put a bag over her head.

"Don't know about that, pizza face, you see you never really figured that far ahead ..." It amused Wayne that she'd had the smarts to think up all these little touches to his plan, but was dumb enough to believe that he'd actually be waiting for her somewhere down the line. Women!

She heard him pick up the bag with the cash, the office door clanging shut behind him.

Susie had expected as much.

She rolled over to her typist's chair, and positioned herself under the seat adjustment lever; the bag over her head hooked off easily. The tricky bit was pulling the phone off the desk so it fell face up. She tugged at the cord, the phone came off the hook and she could see the numbers quite clearly. Although her ankles were bound, she manouevered her long, slim legs over the dial pad; thank goodness all that dancing paid off. Her stilettos picked out the numbers easily: 911.

Five minutes after the call, the police picked up Wayne with the stolen cash sitting in the front seat of his pick-up.

Mr. Jefferson was taken to hospital with a bad concussion and

Susie was being hailed a heroine. Wayne's claim that Susie and he had been in it together, and that she'd planned to meet up with him later, was put down to sour grapes as the whole town knew the girl had rebuffed him weeks ago, and anyway she'd been the one who called the police.

More than the one-way ticket to the county jail, it ate Wayne up no end that the spotty-faced girl had concocted a win-win situation for herself.

What with the handsome reward Mr. Jefferson gave her for foiling the robbery, the money for selling her story to the newspaper, plus her savings, Susie finally had close to $5,000 cash, more than enough to pay for her dermabrasion treatment.

Her getaway was imminent; Susie was ready to hit the big city, dancing, with skin as smooth as the plan she'd carried off.

JEANETTE CLARKE - II

Green

"I want to eat key-lime pie at sunset in the Florida Keys," I'd told Leonard three weeks earlier, in answer to his question what would make me happy.

He was willing to give me the moon, so he was getting off lightly. Leonard owed me that much. After all, he was the one who'd had the affair. He was the one that had a hell of a lot making up to do.

"And what's key-lime pie when it's at home?" Leonard asked, not into desserts and not really interested, period.

"Like lemon meringue, only it's made with limes: it's green," I explained patiently. But I sensed he'd stopped listening.

See, that's the problem with Leonard. He never listens to me anymore. Now is there anything more soul-destroying than when your significant other, he who'd promised to love, honour and obey, can't even be bothered to listen?

Anyhow, here we are in our rented villa in the Florida Keys, waiting to catch the sunset. I've set up the little white wrought iron bistro table and chairs by the pool, a luxury wasted on us since neither of us swim; still it looks impressive in the holiday snaps. Leonard appears with our coffee on a tray.

"Bet you thought I'd forgotten!" he smiles, looking pleased with himself. "Well you wanted to be eating pie, in the Florida Keys at sunset. Your wish is my command, milady!"

Has Leonard actually got it right; must I forgive him yet again, I wonder.

With a flourish, he puts a cup of coffee in front of me, along with a dessert plate containing one giant slice of lemon meringue pie.

"Here comes the sunset." Leonard sits down, sips his coffee and looks to where the sky is changing to orange.

I get up, lean over Leonard and whisper in his ear. With one almighty push he and the chair topple backwards into the pool, the deep end of the pool; the splash is stupendous.

The sky is on fire as I watch the sun set from the wooden jetty. I've been gone about ten minutes. By the time I get back to the villa, Leonard should be dearly departed.

Of course, I'll call 911 and be suitably distraught. I mean, I am upset. I'll sit by the pool waiting for the emergency services to arrive and look at that slice of yellow and gooey lemon meringue pie still sitting on the table.

The last words my late-husband heard would probably make a suitable obituary: "If only you had listened, Leonard: it was key lime pie I wanted, the green one."

JEANETTE CLARKE - III

The Italian Job

I'm an old man now, but I remember every minute of that day, and as time for me grows short, I remember more often.

It's hot outside, and from my basement window I can see my grapes cascading over the trellis: it will be a good year for wine. I can see only the feet of my wife, Lucia, tramping about the grass in her carpet slippers, weeding the flowers, talking to herself. Me, I like to sit in my recliner, a gift from the grandchildren, with all the bells and whistles: a button to raise the footrest, a back massager, it even has a goddam cooler to keep my beer in while I watch the ball game. I tell ya, at my age, it's better than sex!

But when I was young ... I was a soldier in the U.S. army, and only twenty-two when the war finished, and they shipped me back Stateside. I couldn't settle: too much nervous energy, too much testosterone, like a friggin' cat on a hot tin roof. I came from a big close-knit Italian family in Queens, but after six months under their feet, my parents couldn't stand it no more.

"I'm sending you back to the old country to help out your grandfather, Nonno Beppo, on the farm," my papa announced one day. He wanted to protect his interests in the family farm in Italy: there was no arguing with papa.

Three weeks later I was knee-deep in manure in a f•••••• field, wondering what the hell I'd done to deserve this. Exactly a year earlier, I'd been chasing Germans up the boot of Italy, helping to set free one small town after another. I tell ya some of those places were reduced to rubble and I felt bad for the poor Italian peasants we had to leave in that mess; after all these were my people too. That bastard Mussolini deserved everything he got.

I was dog-tired after working the fields with my cousins – ignorant sons-of-bitches. The only thing we had in common was we were all crack shots, and practiced sometimes in the afternoons when it was too hot to work, shooting holes in tin cans till they looked like collanders. After a year though, I'd had enough. Nonno

Beppo wanted to keep me there, and why not, I could work those two no-good cousins of mine under the table. I knew papa wanted me there too, so instead of writing to him I sent a letter to my god-father, Sam, in the States, asking him for help.

There is a code among Italians, and especially in the Mafia; after my godfather intervened to get me brought back home, and set me up in business, I owed him. But he didn't ask too much of me; he had plenty of goons to do any dirty work. I got married, had kids, and after several years got lulled into a false sense of security. I didn't see Sam too often, mainly at big Italian weddings and funerals of course; there were always plenty of funerals. It was at one of these I was summoned in front of the big man himself. I knew it would be a contract.

"This is special," he said. "Can you handle it?" To say no was suicide, after what they'd told me: they'd covered all the details. In the short time I had to prepare I practically lived at the firing range, and made out my will.

Like I said before, that day is etched in my mind: I can go over the details, time and again, as if in slow motion. I had a good vantage point behind the crowds, and afterwards a quick getaway amidst all the confusion. All I had to do really was point and shoot, and there was no problem there: I just kept that little pink pillbox hat directly in my sight and aimed to the left. That's all it came down to on a sunny day in Dallas, November 22, 1963.

So why did you do it, I can hear you ask. For me, it was a debt to be paid, a matter of honour. The presidential family brought it on themselves. They knew the rules when they asked for the votes that put them in office: you don't mess with the Mafia.

It went off without a hitch really. Oswald, Ruby, anyone and everyone who even sniffed at the truth are all gone now. But someone had to be the last man standing, and that man is me, and I will take this secret to my grave.

I've still got the rifle, a Carcano – Italian of course, which I've asked to be buried with me. For someone who changed the course of history, my final resting place will be in a nearby cemetery, a quiet inconspicuous spot, much like the one I chose that long ago day: I will be buried behind a green, grassy knoll.

RICHARD TORPEY - I

Gladys, Angel Intern

"My, she's a pretty one this time," murmured Gladys as she adjusted the wayward feather on her outrageous hat and got up from the waiting room bench in the downtown Toronto bus terminal.

The older gentleman on its other end nearly had a stroke as he believed he had been alone on the bench for the past hour. He did not know, of course, that Gladys only became visible to mortals when she was on duty and her duties today began the exact moment the bus pulled in from out west and Bella got off.

Even though she felt she ought to be doing something much more important at this stage in her career, Gladys smiled as she walked up to Bella because that's what angels are supposed to do at all times, according to the manual, no matter how they feel personally.

She grasped Bella's arm at the very same time as a dandily dressed young man arrived at her side and reached for her suitcase. In a flash, Gladys' hatpin dug deep into his hand and he fell to the ground in pain, uttering a number of words not appropriate for young ears or angels. Just as quickly, the hatpin was returned to its original locale and Gladys had the suitcase instead.

"Come with me, dear," she said pleasantly and started to walk to the taxi stand.

"Hey, wait a minute," said Bella. "Who the heck are you and who is that guy on the ground?"

"Oh, that's Vincent, the fella you have been e-mailing these last few months, who promised you a modelling job if you would come to Toronto and that he would make you a star. You really don't want to know him. And I'm Gladys. I am here to see you don't get into trouble. I am an intern angel sent to you by your dear mother who has been watching over you these past few years. She isn't allowed to come herself and I have been chosen to stand in for her. Come on, let's get us a taxi and get you a place to stay."

"Yeah, sure," snorted Bella. "And I am Queen Victoria. My mother has been gone for five years and I don't believe in angels and all this after-death crap. Now get out of my way. You don't know a damn thing about me."

"You don't think so, dear? Well, then explain to me how come I know your name is Bella, that you come from Peace River, Alberta, that the young man on the ground there bleeding and in very much pain, I hope, is called Vincent, And how do I know that you will turn 19 in four days' time and have exactly $41 in your purse right now?"

Bella was stunned to silence and was in a taxi before she could react. Gladys paid the driver as they arrived at the YWCA on Front Street, smiling even more as she thought about how all she had to do was reach into the old cloth purse she carried and there was everything needed to realise her assignment. For example, here now was the key to Room 427 along with a business card for Angie's Steakhouse, a well-known family restaurant downtown that was looking for young women to waitress. The elevator took them to the fourth floor, Bella in a kind of trance.

Just as they reached Room 427, Bella finally came out of her daze. She dug in her heels, saying, "This is all nonsense. I don't care what you say. I don't believe a word of it. I won't stay here. What makes you think I won't tell people all about you and your crazy hat."

"Because, my dear, as soon as you enter that room, you will remember none of this, including the part where Vincent lured you here. You will not know I was ever part of your life. Tomorrow, you will go to Angie's Steakhouse and you will be hired. In time, you will meet people who will be good to you, helping you to become a solid and loved citizen of society. I see a rather bright young man in your future. All you have to do is open this door. And ... well, I have to ask, what's the matter with my hat?"

Bella ignored the question, shrugging as she turned the doorknob of Room 427. Inside, sitting at a desk, was another young girl with large brown eyes, grinning with pleasure.

She stood up and extended her hand, "Hi, I'm Cory. I'm so glad they found me a roommate at last. You get that bed over there and that bureau. Put your things on it and let's get acquainted. I come from Montreal."

Bella put her suitcase on the bed, then slowly emptied her pockets on the dresser as her new friend looked over her shoulder. With an odd intake of breath, Cory spoke, "Hey, you got one of those hatpin things too, huh?"

RICHARD TORPEY - II

The Bully

All his life, he was called a bully. I don't know who started it or why but that's another story, isn't it? Take my word for it, though, Donnie was no bully. He just looked like and pretended to be one.

In Grade School, he ruled the schoolyard, loving every minute of it. It was his realm. His word was law. If he wanted to play softball, we played softball. If he wanted to play king of the hill, we played king of the hill. If he was inclined to do nothing that day, we did nothing too.

Donnie had his battles, we all did, but never once, not ever, did he have one with anyone smaller or weaker than him. In High School, it was more of the same. People just didn't challenge Donnie since he had grown to be so strong and menacing. He was the school's best defensive end in football and a City All-Star. You don't challenge an All-Star.

For reasons I can't define, though, I was never afraid of Donnie and he knew it. I think it may have been because I saw right through his facade when others did not. A few times when everyone would be trying so hard to please him, he would look at me and wink. In an odd way, although we were never close friends, we shared a secret.

Fast forward to 1953. The years had been kind to me. I had graduated in the top five of my senior class, spent 4 years in college and returned home to a decent job and a pretty girl. Donnie, on the other hand, was not so lucky. He barely graduated, became a garage jockey right out of High School, drank way too much and suffered two disastrous marriages before joining the army; now a proud corporal.

That spring, we met again for the first time since school at the St. Patrick's Day party in the parish hall. He and a stunning blonde were sitting at a table with two empty chairs when I walked in with my soon-to-be bride. When he saw me, he jumped up and yelled at the top of his voice, "Hey Rick, get your ass over here!"

I was actually hoping to sit with friends but it is not easy to refuse Donnie. Besides, I was genuinely happy to see him and looked forward to hearing how he was doing after all this time. And so we sat. I introduced Estelle and looked at Donnie questioningly about the blonde. It took him awhile to get it and then I wished he hadn't because the next sentence out of his mouth went something like this.

"Yeah, well, this is ab...this is ab...this is ab...What the hell is your name anyway?" The blonde never batted an eye as she told us her name was Yvonne.

It was St. Paddy's Day after all and we did what every good old Irish lad had been doing for ages. We drank, we sang and we laughed. Then we drank, sang and laughed some more. Something was not right, though. Donnie was avoiding my eyes; and when the band began playing "Danny Boy" for the seventh time, he looked at me and got very serious.

'Rick," he said, choosing his words carefully so that he was sure

I would hear him amidst the bedlam around us, "I'm really not as dumb as people think, you know. Maybe I'm not smart like you, but I'm not stupid either. I'm a damn good soldier for one thing. I know what people think of me. And I know you've been too polite to ask me why I joined the army so I'll tell you. Not many people know this. Being a soldier has always been my dream; ever since I was a little boy. My Ma hated everything military so I didn't do it until she passed away. Now I'm happy at last. And I'll tell you something else not many people know, Ricky boy. We ship out to Korea on Monday morning and I won't be coming back."

I was stunned for a minute, then blurted. "Look, Donnie, I'm really happy for you, honestly. I think you did the right thing. But after Korea, where the hell do you think you'll go? This is your home. Come back here where you know everyone and things will work out. As you said, you're not stupid. You'll make it."

Donnie looked blank for a moment and then, "You don't get it, do you Rick? When I say I'm not coming back, I don't mean I'm going somewhere else. I mean I won't be coming back."

He got up and walked away. I don't remember much about the rest of the evening or how I got home that night.

I never saw Donnie alive again. He had it right. He left for Korea that Monday morning as scheduled and came back two months later in a flag-draped coffin.

The story I heard was that he ordered the remnants of his platoon to retreat when they were completely overrun by Chinese regulars on a ridge, ironically called "Heartache". He was the only NCO left and they obeyed him as they always did when he gave an order. He stayed behind to cover them. Twenty-nine men lived to fight another day but one good man did not.

I attended Donnie's funeral and drove behind the hearse to the cemetery. I listened to the Army Padre recite all the right prayers and swallowed hard when the time came for his coffin to be lowered into the ground. At that very moment, not one second before or not one second after, I suddenly understood what Donnie had told me two months before. Donnie's dream was not to be a soldier. THIS was his dream.

I looked around at the faces of the mourners at his gravesite and saw something there I had seen so many times before when Donnie was with us. I was ashamed for them and for me. And so I yelled, in a voice I hardly recognized, what no newspaperman there had the courage to print the next day,

"HE WAS NOT A BULLY. HE WAS NEVER A BULLY!"

And with tears staining my jacket, I ran to my car and to the rest of my life.

RICHARD TORPEY - III

Rail Tales

My stupid, older brother dropped me off at the station 20 minutes after my train left. Of course, I didn't know that until I walked into the small building and found Mr. Hurley, the stationmaster, down on his knees ready to put the day's receipts in the safe.

He looked up at me quizzically and asked what I thought I was doing there at this time of night. When I told him I had a ticket to Windsor on the 9:10, he gave me the bad news.

"That train left 20 minutes ago, son. There's not another one coming through here till the morning. In fact, there ain't another train due to stop here all night long and I'm closing up. You'll have to go home."

"I can't go home, sir. My brother's gone already. He didn't even get out of the car. And I live 60 miles from here. Even if he goes right home, which I doubt, it'll be morning before he can come get me. I'll stay right here, sir, if it's alright with you."

Mr. Hurley gummed about this for a short while, then let out a long sigh. As if he were afraid of being overheard, he whispered, "Okay, you can stay inside here till morning but I can't leave the lights on and you got to be quiet as a mouse. I'd take you home with me 'cept the missus is ailing again and carrying on. I'll be back by early morning. You got to promise me no one will ever know about this, hear?" I nodded and he left muttering, locking the door behind him.

There are times a 12-year old boy pretends to be brave but being alone in a dark railroad station at night is not one of them.

Within a few minutes of the sound of Mr. Hurley's car leaving, I began to shake and cry softly. I was scared beyond any normal sense. When I heard a key being turned in the lock again, my first thought was that Mr. Hurley had returned for some reason. But, almost immediately, my brain told me I had not heard his car.

Terror gripped me as the door opened and a large shape blocked the lighter gloom of the outside. The door closed and I was once more in complete darkness, only this time I was not alone.

A soft, raspy voice devoid of malice came from across the room. "Don't be frightened, young lad. My name is Sam Hawkins and I live here ... Well, not really. I sleep here the nights no trains stop. I don't have a place of my own, wouldn't you know, and this is as good a place as any. The railroad people don't know about me so far and I'm hoping you won't be telling them, eh?"

I was too stunned to speak, so Sam continued, "I suppose you must be wondering about me, eh? Well, the truth is I worked for this here railroad all my life in one job or another. That's why I have a key. When they retired me, I had no place to go. My poor old quarters had burned to the ground in '76 and my retirement pay wasn't good enough to build again. So I live in the woods near Connor's Cove in the daytime and sleep here at night when I can. So, what do you think of that?"

I made several attempts to say something intelligent but the long silences were too much for Sam. "OK then, I'll do the talking and you can try to sleep. I wish I had the schooling to write a book about the rail for there's a heap of stories I could tell, believe me. For example, did you ever hear about when trains had cowcatchers? They were those odd looking grille things on the front of the engine to knock loose stuff off the tracks.

"Well, wouldn't you know, one day when I was working up front, we actually picked up a REAL cow! We had to stop and let her off. Not a scratch on her. She waddled off into the field chewing her cud like blazes, looking at us with scorn. We never told the passengers what the delay was. And the time Tommy Two Oaks got into the shine and came aboard with a bow and arrow, threatening to scalp any white folks that said anything to him. I was the conductor on that trip and I had to remind him that a bow and arrow don't scalp so good. He thought about that for awhile and then fell asleep in the aisle. People had to jump over him for the rest of his trip to St. Thomas.

"I don't think I'll ever forget the newlywed couple that got on in Oshawa and the little bride never stopped crying all the way to Windsor. The poor groom had no idea what to do. Looked like he wanted to cry himself. Never did find out if they made a go of it.

"Starting to get sleepy? Well, go right ahead, I'll just keep talking here. Don't get a lot of chance to do much of it at Connor's Cove, that's for sure."

And indeed, his calm voice had erased all traces of my fear and I fell asleep clad in its warmth. When I awoke, the first rays of sunlight coming through the side window told me I was alone again.

When Mr. Hurley arrived, I asked if he knew a Sam Hawkins without giving away that he was there overnight. He replied as if it were a reasonable question.

"Of course I do, lad. Sam's a strange one. Never married. Lives in the woods over by Connor's Cove. Best fisherman in these parts. Keeps telling folks he wishes he had a son to pass on his fishing skills. Damn shame, I say."

I went to Windsor that morning and thought about Sam most of the way. I don't know why, but I knew somehow that brief meeting would direct my life. On my return, I made a pilgrimage to Connor's Cove a week later and Sam and I became fast friends.

Over the years, I went back many times. We would sit by the stream when not actually in it up to our hip boots and his stories of the railroad would flow as did the water itself; some comic, some tragic, all of keen interest to a young boy, growing up.

I know one day I will write about Sam and his tales for this has been my choice of careers. I don't know who adopted who.

I can only tell you I became a pretty darn good fisherman while Sam had himself a son until the day he left this world for a far better fishing hole.

KONRAD BRINCK - I

The Incredible Lives Of My Two Uncle Willies

Technically, neither one of my two Uncle Willies was my uncle. Uncle Willie in Ebstorf was my father's cousin and the one in Potsdam was my grandmother's youngest brother. Both of them were named Wilhelm Totzke. It is customary in Germany to address older relatives as uncle or aunt. My father was very close to both, since he spent part of his childhood with them in Pomerania, now part of Poland.

Their lives were remarkable and I wasn't aware of their stories until I visited them later in my life and they talked about the tumultuous and unbelievable hardships they had to endure.

Here are the stories they told me.

Uncle Willie In Potsdam

When my wife Jackie and I visited Germany in 1975, we visited Uncle Willie, his wife Aunt Minna and their family in Neu Fahrland near Potsdam in East Germany. Uncle Willie had broken his collarbone and was bedridden. On a rainy day, he called us into his bedroom to chat. He was intrigued by Jackie and her African heritage and was eager to find out what life in Africa was like.

He spoke no English and I translated his questions and Jackie's answers all morning. After a while he asked if we would be interested in hearing his life story after lunch. It turned out to be one of the most fascinating days of our lives.

Uncle Willie enjoyed the schnapps I had brought from West Berlin to make the day more pleasant but made sure that Aunt Minna didn't find out that he was enjoying the brandy along with the stories. She did not approve of his drinking during the day or, for that matter, at any time of the day. His timing in telling the story of his life was impeccable. He stopped every couple of minutes for me to translate and used that time to relight or refill his pipe and have a little sip of brandy to wet his throat.

Uncle Willie was born in 1892 and spent his childhood and youth in Pomerania. His first job was as a stable boy on one of Kaiser Wilhelm's estates. He met the Kaiser and had good memories of the days in his employment.

During the first World War, he joined the infantry and fought at the battle of the Marne. He took part in the trench warfare for over two years. The hardship and savagery almost broke him. He talked about fellow soldiers dying next to him in their foxholes, or while advancing or retreating during the constant attacks and counter-attacks.

It was hard for me to find the words in English to express the horror and the suffering he and every soldier on both sides had to endure, but Jackie understood by his animated gestures and the tears now running down his face. We had a hard time hiding our own tears as we watched him reliving those days. When he returned from the war he was rehired by the new owner of the estate and through the years of the Weimar Republic he was quite happy living in Pomerania. He married Minna and his only daughter Ilse was born in 1933.

When Hitler came to power he noticed that Jews were disappearing from the nearby town of Rummelsburg. Hitler's Brown Shirts also intimidated and terrorized people who refused to join the Nazi Party and many were incarcerated or vanished. The owner of the estate, who was part of the old German aristocracy and not a Nazi sympathizer, fled to the United States in 1939 after the war broke out. The Nazis confiscated the estate and ran it until the end of the war.

Uncle Willy, due to his age, was only drafted into the army during the final months of the Second World War and was captured by the Russians on the Eastern Front.

He returned from the prisoner of war camp, where he suffered from the cold and lack of food, to his wife and daughter in the early winter of 1945 only to find out that Pomerania was now Polish territory. Germans who did not want to take Polish citizenship were forced to leave. The use of the German language was outlawed and he and his family envisioned a life as second class citizens if they decided to stay.

They, along with thousands of others, were rounded up and and told to take only the belongings they could carry and leave Poland. The elderly, children, the sick and the able bodied had to march for twelve hours a day in the middle of winter to reach the new German border more than 230 km away.

The few hand-drawn carts in this convoy of humanity loaded with personal belongings could only accommodate a few people who had collapsed or were unable to walk. The Soviet and Polish soldiers driving the people towards the border showed no mercy towards those who couldn't find a place on the carts and were unable to continue. They either executed them with a single bullet to the head or simply bashed their skull in with the butt of their rifles and left them lying by the side of the road.

The hatred towards Germans exhibited by many Poles and Russians at the end of the war was without limits and the feeling of revenge and payback for the atrocities committed during the Third Reich justified their actions in their minds.

When Uncle Willie described these scenes we were all crying

uncontrollably and had to stop at times to regain our composure.

He arrived in West Berlin and tried to start a new life. Since his experience was in agriculture, the only work he could find was clearing rubble and other jobs to rebuild a city in ruins. Aunt Minna had relatives near Potsdam who owned a small farm. They introduced my uncle to Mrs. Wartenberg, who owned a large estate close-by in the village of Neu Fahrland. She had lost her husband in the war and was looking for a live-in farmhand to assist her and her young son Werner. Uncle Willie and Aunt Minna accepted her offer and moved to East Germany in early 1950.

There were three houses on the Wartenberg property. Mother Wartenberg and her son Wernie, as everybody called him, occupied the main building. The second house belonged to Wernie's sister and her family. The third, and biggest house, was now the home of Uncle Willie, Tante Minna and Ilse.

As Ilse grew up to be a lovely young lady, she and Wernie fell in love with each other. They got married in 1953 and moved into the main building to occupy the quarters on the ground floor. The upstairs was converted into a self contained apartment for Mother Wartenberg to live in.

Everybody seemed to be happy. Then, in 1954, the Communist East German government nationalised all farms and converted them into state owned cooperatives. Uncle Willie and Wernie now lived in state owned houses and were employees of the East German Government.

At the end of our long day listening to Uncle Willie's life story, I had to ask him the following question, "Tell me Uncle Willie, you have lived under all imaginable forms of government, from the monarchy of Kaiser Wilhelm, to the unruly democracy of the Weimar Republic, to a dictatorship under Hitler, to a western style democracy in West Berlin and finally Communism in East Germany. Which form of government did you like the best?"

His answer surprised me. "Konrad," he said, "now in my old age I feel secure and know that my family and I are well looked after. I can die in peace knowing my grandchildren will get a good education, they will be guaranteed a job for the rest of their lives and will never starve. I know we are lacking a lot of freedoms and will never live in luxury but peace of mind means a lot after what

Minna and I have gone through in our lives. I must say that Communism is, maybe, the most desirable form of government."

I didn't agree with him but, in a way, I understood.

In 1975, when we visited for the first time, there were four generations living on the farm. Mother Wartenberg, Uncle Willie and Aunt Minna, their children Wernie and Ilse, their daughter Bärbel with her husband Manfred and their son Michael. After Michael got married to his wife Yvonne, that number increased to five generations living under the same roof when their son Julius was born in 2003. Mother Wartenberg died at the age of 99 in 2006.

Uncle Willie died before German reunification and never experienced his family flourishing in a free society on their again-privately owned estate.

Uncle Willie in Ebstorf

I only met Uncle Willie in 1958. He and his wife Ilse and their six children were living on a farm in Velgen in Lower Saxony, West Germany.

Uncle Willie and his family had been trapped in Poland after the war and my father was eager to see his cousin, whom I called Uncle Willie, again after more than 20 years. Uncle Willie's father-in-law was the manager, administrator and all-round, go-to man of the local dairy farm and creamery. He and Uncle Willie had managed the farm and the creamery throughout the war years and the Polish government would not allow them or their families to leave Pomerania to follow the rest of the Totzke clan to West Germany.

Only after his father in law died in 1957 and Ilse's brother, a farmer in West Germany, sponsored them to leave Poland, were they finally allowed to take their few belongings and board a train to West Berlin.

Uncle Willie was born in Pomerania in 1920 and married Ilse in 1940 shortly before their first daughter Dora was born later that same year. Eight more children were to follow. In 1938, Uncle Willie joined the police force in Pomerania as a cadet. After he completed basic training, he was shipped to France in 1940 to police Paris as a member of the occupying force. After the Vichy government was installed by the Germans, some autonomy was returned to the French, including local policing. German police were slowly replaced by their French counterparts and by the middle of 1941 the last German police officers were decommissioned. Uncle Willie and others were given a choice, they could either join the regular army and be shipped to the Eastern Front or join the SS and be deployed behind the lines to fight local resistance groups or do other non combat duties.

Very few accepted the offer to fight at the Eastern Front to face the Russians and the upcoming brutal winter.

After his basic training in the SS, he was assigned to fight the Yugoslavian Resistance Movement, one of the most feared and successful anti-Nazi movements during the Second World War.

He became friends with an Austrian named Anton, who had also been part of the police force in France and resented the war just as much as Uncle Willie did. One day they were lying in a foxhole when Anton said, "I heard these Partisans are pretty good sharpshooters. So what do you think if we wave at them? They will shoot us in the arm, we'll go home and the war is over for us."

Uncle Willie argued that it would not be good to be shot in the hand as they'd be crippled for life. "No, no," Anton answered, "if you wave really fast your upper arm is hardly moving and they always aim for the part that is not moving as fast." He raised his arm to demonstrate hoping to be only slightly injured.

What neither Anton nor Uncle Willie knew was that the Partisan a few meters away was not a good shot at all but had a great arm and could toss a hand grenade a long way. Now knowing where the enemy was hiding, that is exactly what he did and for Uncle Willie and his friend Anton the war was now over.

Anton was badly injured, but survived. Uncle Willie lost the heel of his left foot and had many shrapnel wounds. He walked with a limp for the rest of his life. After two months in hospital, he was discharged and returned home. Upon his return to Pomerania, he had to start a new life. His dreams of being a policeman were over. He started working with his father-in-law at the dairy and quickly became an expert in all aspects of dairy farming.

When Uncle Willie's family was denied permission to leave Poland, he lived in constant terror that the Polish authorities would find out about him being part of the SS. In the early days after the war, members of the SS were routinely charged with war crimes or simply executed by the Soviets without a trial. When joining the SS, all recruits were required to be tattooed for identification purposes. After the war, that tattoo under their left arm made them easily recognizable. Most SS members had their tattoos removed or simply cut out but scars were an obvious giveaway. Uncle Willie always wore a shirt in order to conceal the fact that he was part of Hitler's elite troop that was responsible for most of the atrocities committed by Germans during the Third Reich.

I still remember meeting Uncle Willie and his family in 1958. My father had fond memories of taking him under his wing and introducing him to all the mischievous things teenagers could get into, mainly alcohol, tobacco and girls. Dad, seven years older than his cousin, must have done a good job because the reunion was a weekend long affair with lots of booze, smoking and stories about the past.

Uncle Willie's six children were proof that Dad had definitely taught him well about the art of love-making. I had a great weekend as well. Uncle Willie spent a long time teaching me how to ride a horse bareback. There were no saddles on the farm and after a few lessons, I became pretty good. I had a great time riding around pretending to be the greatest cowboy to ever sat on a horse. It wasn't until the next day that I discovered that every bone in my body was hurting and I could hardly walk.

After settling down in Germany, Uncle Willie and Tante Ilse had three more children. They bought a small house in nearby Ebstorf and life finally looked like there would only be happy days ahead of them. Shortly after their last daughter Ute was born in 1966, the doctors gave them some terrible news. Tante Ilse had cancer and and was told that she had less than a year to live.

She died in 1968 and Uncle Willie was left with eight children to look after. His oldest daughter Dora was married and had moved out of the house a few years earlier.

Uncle Willie picked himself up and reorganized his life to be a father and a mother. He had all his children complete their education and helped them develop the skills to succeed in life. Nobody enjoyed life more than Uncle Willie. His bellicose laugh, his permanent smile and his positive outlook on life made him a joy to be around. Even though he never wanted to get married again, he loved the ladies and had some girlfriends after his wife died.

My mother told me that he even tried to seduce her when she came to visit him after my father died. When she reminded him that she was six years older than him and widowed, he said, "You are never too old to have a good time and you shouldn't live your life for the dead. They'll forgive you when you meet them in heaven again."

Uncle Willie never gave up trying to charm the ladies around him but struck out with my mother.

In 1990, we toured Germany with friends of ours, Joan and Willis, who were originally from Barbados. Uncle Willie had never had contact with black people before in his life and was fascinated with Joan, a stunning and beautiful black woman. When we left. she kissed him on the cheek. One of his sons told us later that he didn't wash his face for over a week after the kiss. He said he didn't want to wash the memories away of having been kissed by such a gorgeous woman.

On that visit, he also taught our then 16-year-old daughter Toni how to do shots of his homemade liqueur. Jackie and I were stunned when we saw that Toni downed a few of them to my uncle's delight. He said his plum and herbal mixture wouldn't hurt her. I guess he was right because Toni had a good night's sleep and didn't wake up until early afternoon the next day after wobbling off to bed the night before.

Whenever we went to Germany we always tried to visit him and his children, most of whom were married and living around Ebstorf. His daughter Gisela and her husband George as well as his son Ullie, his wife Anka and their son have visited us several times in Canada.

Uncle Willie died suddenly in 1999 of a heart attack at the age of 79. Even though I spent very little time with him over the years, he will always be one of my favourite relatives.

Nobody could resist his charm, his smile and his enthusiasm. He was a pleasure to be around.

KONRAD BRINCK - II

The Beginning

I have never met Dora nor do I know what she looked like but she is the main reason for me being born into this world.

Nobody in our family ever talked about Dora and I only became aware of her existence after my father's death when my mother confided in me about her not-always picture-perfect marriage to my father.

I have often thought of my father sitting in a cold and dark barrack, barely lit by the midnight sun in northern Norway where he was stationed during WWII. He wrote regularly to my mother and she was always looking forward to his loving words and shared his desire to be back in each other's arms again.

When she received another letter in the summer of 1944 expressing these sentiments and declaring his undying love for her there was only one problem, it wasn't addressed to her but to a women named Dora. My mother had no idea who Dora was but it became increasingly clear to her that she was my father's mistress and that she received the letter that was meant for Dora.

The approaching British planes, the twilight of the midnight sun, the rush to take up positions at the anti-aircraft guns or quickly trying to get his letters into the army post box, who knows what caused this moment of lack of attention to detail. Anybody could have switched the letters with the envelopes by mistake.

Just a dumb mistake! But it surely changed everybody's life.

My mother must have been in shock when she read that my father had the same feelings for this other woman that he had expressed for her and she was waiting for him to return home from the front in order to end their marriage and start a new life without him. Could she perhaps find a way to forgive him? Would he show any remorse and want to continue a life together.

My mother had to wait almost a year to confront my father. The mixed feelings and uncertainty took a big toll on her life. The long nights sitting in the bomb shelter in Berlin while bombs rained all over the city, gave her lots of time to contemplate her future if she and her husband should survive this war.

My father didn't return until June of 1945 after having been a POW for a short time. He feared the scene and confrontation that was waiting for him. He had a whole year to prepare for it and must have gone over it in his mind again and again. Dora let him know that she received the letter adressed to my mother and, according to my father, she stopped the affair almost immediately. She was shocked to learn that there was a Mrs Brinck waiting for him upon his return.

There is one thing I inherited from my father and that is his gift of the gab and being very persuasive.

I have no idea what he said to my mother and how much begging he had to do for her to take him back and forgive him for his indiscretion, but he succeeded. My mother was a very forgiving and loving person but she insisted on one thing in order to continue her life with him, a child.

My parents had long given up on the idea of having another child after their first son, Harry, born in 1932 with a heart defect, lived only for 5 weeks, after doctors said they could not save him.

A second child was stillborn in 1936 and my parents gave up hope of ever experiencing the joys of parenthood. They agreed to live a life as a couple, devoted to each other and find happiness outside the confines of parenthood to avoid further heartbreaks.

Dora changed all that. They agreed to try one more time to have a child in order to cement a marriage in trouble.

After a short time, my mother got pregnant and in July of 1946, I was born. I certainly kept my part of the bargain by keeping them together for the rest of their lives. I hope to have given them what they were looking for, happiness!

I would really like to thank Dora, but I don't think she is still alive and possibly never knew that her affair with a young German soldier ended up in making a family happy and making her responsible for the existence of a pretty terrific human being,

Me!

KONRAD BRINCK - III

A Goodbye to Daisy

A long time ago, I remember the day
you came for a visit and started to play.
You were nibbling my ear and licking my nose
I tickled your belly and was holding you close.

> You felt soft and fluffy and looked really cute
> I'd chase you around, you'd run, skip and scoot
> you sat in my lap and then peed on my shoe
> and that was the moment I knew I loved you.

We slept in my bed when you stayed for the night;
You enjoyed the wild games and squealed with delight;
after playing, we'd cuddle and then fall asleep;
you slept until morning, not making a peep.

> We went for long walks, I let you run free;
> you loved chasing birds or squirrels up a tree;
> you never gave up but never caught one;
> and what if you did, what would you have done?

You'd sit next to me when I sat down to eat
and beg for eight pieces of chicken or meat;
you'd even eat veggies or breaded fried fish,
but ignored your own food, served in your own dish.

> As you grew older there was no more joy;
> you hardly played with me or touched any toy;
> you had a bad cough and trouble when walking;
> you didn't hear doorbells or noises or talking.

I know little Daisy has left us today!
in doggie heaven she'll be happy and play;
and I am quite certain that she will try
to finally catch that butterfly. Goodbye Daisy!

MARGARET HOLLYWELL - I

Snakes Alive!

We knew Grandma Ryan had problems when she started seeing snakes. She saw snakes in her dining room, in her living room and in her bedroom. Some slithered across the floor near her feet, others stuck their heads through knotholes and hissed. Whenever a scream rattled the boards at Grandma's, we all rushed over from Uncle Mike's house next door to see what was wrong.

"What is it, Grandma?"

" I just saw a snake crawling across the floor!"

"Where is it now?"

"It just went through that knothole."

Grandma was tiny and wizened, white-haired and ninety years old. Her most cheerful smile couldn't hide all the wrinkles in her face but ever since I remember she'd helped me with my problems. She would solve them and give me the benefit of her wisdom. It didn't seem right that she should be acting this way. She was so kind, it was sad to think that her mind might be slipping.

But Aunt Hannah saw things differently. "It's all her own fault," she would say, standing in the doorway of the kitchen like a preacher. Aunt Hannah loved to preach.

"She drinks booze and sees imaginary snakes. Claims the whisky relieves her arthritis. I think it relieves her of her senses."

Grandma lived alone in her old run-down, east of town home. The house needed paint and the roof leaked. Still, in summer, her tiny garden was a riot of colour. Her roses were gone to pot, over-blown and fat, but the sweet smelling jasmine had taken over. We'd asked her to live with us but Grandma refused. She said Uncle Mike and Aunt Hannah were too particular.

I had to agree with her on that. I'd lived with them for seven years - ever since Dad and Ma died when I was six - so I knew first hand. But strict though they were, I figured I had a good home. Aunt Hannah treated me like a son and Uncle Mike taught me woodworking and polishing.

"You're sorta skinny, kid," he said one day as he sucked on his old blackened pipe, "but you're gonna be able to make a living some day."

Uncle Mike was a big, tall man, but he had trouble with his blood pressure and when he worked too hard he'd sit in the shade and cool off. He was unselfish and didn't want to worry Aunt Hannah about his condition, so we made a pact that I wasn't to talk about it around her. She worried enough as it was.

She worried about me because I had Grandma's smile, an earthly trait that Aunt Hannah considered wicked. She spent hours teaching me right from wrong. She explained that since she'd been baptized by Pastor Benson, she lived above sin. She only liked what was righteous and everything she disliked was evil. She was a Soldier of the Cross who felt called upon to keep people in line. She allowed that Grandma needed more keeping in line than anybody.

"Look at her!" Aunt Hannah's eyebrows almost touched her hair-line! "It's not enough that she drinks and sees snakes, but she has to have her hair curled too!" Aunt Hannah wore hers done up in a tight little ball behind her head.

Grandma started telling her snake stories at the old Baptist Church on Main Street where we sat every Sunday to sing 'Rock of Ages' and to hear Pastor Benson preach. This embarrassed Aunt Hannah. "What'll my friends think!" Aunt Hannah muttered under her breath. "We can't take her with us again." I knew for sure that next Sunday Grandma would not be along, but I think I was more disappointed about it than she was.

Pastor was a skimpy-haired little preacher with a rough complexion. His face was as red as a ripe tomato and a nose like Rudolph the Reindeer. He preached against the evils of the demon rum, the foolishness of those who gave too little money to the church and those who gave nothing at all. He preached against pretty girls in skimpy bathing suits and got so worked up that flecks of saliva issued from his mouth. He fairly breathed fire and brimstone.

He visited the sick - the saints and sinners alike. He consoled ailing saints with the promise of a better home awaiting in the sky. He converted sinners by explaining how God had stricken them for their wickedness. Helping people was more fun to him than sopping up his Irish stew with soda bread. Now he was all set on helping us and insisted on doing something about Grandma.

"You should take her to that doctor at Pine Hills. I'll come by next Tuesday and we can go in my car."

Tuesday morning, since school was out, I went with Grandma, Pastor Benson. Uncle Mike and Aunt Hannah to see the doctor. Well, Grandma was in the doctor's office about an hour.

Then, the doctor called us in. "D'you know your mother drinks?" he asked Uncle Mike.

"Yeah. She takes a toddy morning and night for arthritis."

"She says she takes half a pint a day! For a person her size, that's too much. She's suffering from delirium tremens, characterized by hallucinations. With DT's some people see elephants, some see rats and so on. She sees snakes. So the less she drinks the less snakes she'll see. It's that simple."

All the way home Pastor Benson preached to Grandma. "Shame on you! You're at death's door and drinking the Devil's brew."

"S'not brew! It's good Irish whisky."

"You're not only suffering from drink, you're sending your soul to Hell!"

"Whisky's good medicine and I've used it all my life. I gave it to my babies to ward off the fever."

"The greater sin you've committed. I'd rather see a child wracked with fever than put that stuff in his mouth."

When we got home, Aunt Hannah ranted and raved. "She's a disgrace to us all! She ought to be sent off for treatment."

"Now Hannah ..." Uncle Mike got no further.

"Be quiet while I'm talking!" Uncle Mike never got to finish a sentence when Aunt Hannah was raging. "I don't know who's bringing her that stuff, but I'll find out."

I knew. Every day when Uncle Mike and Aunt Hannah took their afternoon nap, I made a trip on the sly to the corner where Deacon Smith lived. Aunt Hannah would have a fit is she knew he kept a supply.

That night I didn't want any supper. I went to bed early but couldn't sleep for worrying about Grandma. There she was sinning and I was helping her to do it. If I didn't know better there might be a chance of getting forgiveness. But I had to face the facts. I was going back on Aunt Hannah's teaching. I vowed I'd never go again for Grandma's whisky.

I prayed for help - not for myself, but for Grandma. I felt that I might live to atone for my sins but Grandma didn't have much time left and no way of making up for her drinking. It'd take a lot to save her soul.

The next day, I tried not to look at Grandma's house but by noon I couldn't stand it. While things were quiet, I walked over to see her.

"I have an errand for you," she said. Here was a chance to start atoning for my sins, I was the only link between Grandma and the whisky and I could stop her from drinking. Aunt Hannah would be proud of me on Judgement day.

I looked at Grandma's twisted hands and remembered the cookies and cakes she used to make for me. I looked at her stooped shoulders and thought of the time she moved into my room when I was sick with fever. Nobody else would come near me in fear of catching the disease.

Then, I looked up into her bright blue eyes. A twinkle was still there, and she winked at me. I was melted putty! Sure, I'd get the whisky for her and let her go to Hell!

In bed that night I thought about Grandma. Grandma was going to Hell and I was going with her. It didn't matter though, with Grandma there, Hell might not be such a bad place after all.

In the weeks that followed, Pastor Benson practically lived at

Grandma's. He preached and prayed and pleaded, but Grandma kept on drinking her whisky.

"I'm at my wits end," Pastor Benson said. "We may need medical help." Gloom weighed me down when he said that. I'd give anything for Grandma not to be tortured by the sight of snakes, but come Sunday afternoon when she asked me to go for whisky, I couldn't refuse.

Next morning, when I came down for breakfast, they were discussing Grandma again. "Let's send her to the County hospital," said Aunt Hannah.

"But she'd be locked up," said Uncle Mike.

"So be it," prayed Pastor Benson, baptizing another doughnut in his coffee. "If she is locked up, she can't get to the whisky. I'd rather spend the rest of my days locked up and go to heaven, than die in sin." I never saw a man so hell-bent on going to heaven.

"I'll give it one more try," said Pastor Benson, "but time is short. If I can save her soul it'll be another star in my crown." He'd so many stars in his crown now, it'd take a mule to haul it!

On Wednesday evening, Uncle Mike and I went to Grandma's. Pastor Benson's old Ford was parked in front; he was inside preaching to her. As we started along the walk a piercing scream split the air. We rushed into the house and saw Grandma standing over Pastor Benson. He was bent double in a chair - moaning and groaning and holding his leg.

"What happened to him?" Uncle Mike asked.

"Snake bit him." Grandma pointed to a corner of the room. "There he goes! Get him!"

I grabbed a poker and slammed it down on the head of a harmless garden snake that was just about to slide into a knothole.

"I'll get the doctor," said Uncle Mike.

"Never mind," shouted Grandma. "I've got good medicine here," she headed for the cabinet.

I started outside with the snake draped over the poker. When I reached the door, I heard Grandma saying, "Here! Easy! Take it easy with that stuff!"

And there was Pastor Benson taking a powerful drink from Grandma's whisky bottle.

MARGARET HOLLIWELL - II

The Way Of The Irish

GALWAY.

January 6th 1839 was a very curious day. It was what the Irish called a 'saft' (soft) day. Although snow had fallen the night before, by noon the sun on that day had become unseasonably warm. It was Epiphany Sunday and most of the men folk were standing near the crossroads conjecturing about the weather and what, if anything, it would mean, maybe an omen?

The women had no time for comment as they were busy preparing any savoury dishes they could afford to scrape together for the evening celebration. Festive occasions were few and far between, these days. Mostly, it was the sound of a funeral dirge that had become all too familiar. Food was almost non-existent. The roofs of houses had caved in, leaving only a few corners in which to shelter. The potato famine was at its height.

Bridget Reilly stood in the shadow of Mount Dun Aengus looking over the sea while the distant lightning lit up the sky. She was saying 'goodbye' to Innismore and going over the sea to America to join her brother, Cavan. At 16, she was beautiful. Her hair fell in a tumult of red waves and curls. She was thin, but with the shortage of food that was understandable. Memory returned to haunt her and the horror of that night a few weeks ago.

"We need some more turf for the fire," her father had said, moving his muscular frame from the only chair they possessed.

"Here, let me get it." Bridget moved from the fire where she had been stirring a pot with some thin potato soup in it. Outside, the moon was rising and shed a brilliant light over the land. It was a cold night with the promise of frost by morning. She hurried in again with the last two pieces of turf and placed one of them on the fire. It was just a one-room house as were the most of the Irish homes around Galway. Four walls and a roof was the most anyone could afford. Just as she was about to stir the pot again, a noise near the door got her attention.

"Oh, Holy Mother!" she cried out and crossed herself.

"What is it?" her father turned around.

"The picture! Our Blessed Lord! His picture just fell off the wall."

"It must be the damp. You know what it's like this time of year." He placed his pipe between his teeth.

"It's a bad omen for us Da, you know how Mam used to say that when a picture falls off the wall someone's going to die."

"Old wives' tales," he said and turned back to the fire to light his pipe. But Bridget couldn't be persuaded. She'd seen it happen before.

The following night the house was full of neighbours. Everyone who had food to spare brought something with them. Old stories were told and songs were sung. Someone always brought a fiddle and a tin whistle. Suddenly, in the midst of toe tapping and hand clapping, everything went silent.

"Listen, hush now," said one old hag. The women and some of the men crossed themselves as they heard the baying and howling of a dog. This was another omen that the figure of death was abroad in the village.

The next night as Bridget lay on her bed, she heard it again and the following night once more. There was no denying it, three times as the legend proclaimed; when a dog howled three times, death wasn't far behind. She couldn't imagine who it might be, maybe her best friend's old granny? Or maybe Padriac, their neighbour, he was about 90 years old.

The final blow came a few days later when Bridget set a meagre meal of potatoes in front of her father. He had spent the day at the edge of the sea collecting the kelp that he hoped to sell at the Friday market. He was recalling the amount of kelp he'd gathered when he suddenly stopped talking and clutched his chest. Bridget watched in horror as he slumped to the floor.

Then she heard the loud wailing of the Banshee. Some people vowed they had seen a Banshee but most folks thought that was very unlucky. There was no denying that everybody had heard it.

Bridget was brought back to the present as a rattle of thunder rolled across the clouds.

Her Aunt and Uncle had grudgingly taken her in; but with their own five kids she knew she wasn't welcome and was treated like a servant. Having saved up the money her brother had sent her she was ready to leave. She'd dreamed of the day she would join him in America and now it was here. Her best friend Peggy Connelly was going with her. The streets of America hadn't been paved with gold as predicted, only filth and refuse abounded. But she was sure she could make a better life for herself eventually.

MARGARET HOLLIWELL - III

It's An Ill Wind...

Tessa ran as fast as she could and just made the elevator doors as they were closing. Her breath came in gasps as she grabbed the rail inside to lean on.

"Are you alright?" the only other passenger inquired.

Tessa looked up and into the greenest eyes she'd ever seen. His hair was a copper colour and fell in waves over his forehead.

"Sorry," she replied, "I was late for work and didn't want to miss the ride. I'll be okay now as soon as I get my breath back."

"What floor are you going to?" Green Eyes asked.

"Twenty four... it's a long way. Thanks." He punched the button and off they went into the skies. There was an embarrassing silence for a while as Tessa smoothed down her coat and hitched the shoulder strap of her purse into place.

"By the way, my name's Mike Donovan." He held out his hand. Tessa blushed but replied, "I'm Tessa Morgan. I'm just new here so I don't want to create a bad impression."

"Well, sometimes things don't work out the way we want them," Mike said. "I've had mornings like that too."

Suddenly, the elevator gave a few hefty shudders and stopped. Tessa was jolted against Mike who put out his arm to steady her.

She blushed, and steadied herself again with the rail.

"I wonder what's up?" she said. Mike looked at the floor button board. Nothing seemed amiss but they had definitely stopped going up.

"I'll try this button, it says emergency." He pushed and somewhere in the distance a bell could be heard ringing. "That should get some attention."

"Oh dear, I'm not very good at being closed in small spaces." Tessa began to have a panic attack.

"Don't worry," said Mike. "I'm sure whoever heard the bell will call security and we'll be out of here in no time." But the time passed and Tessa became more agitated. Mike put his arm around her and tried to calm her. Finally, she responded and breathed more easily.

"When they let us out of here, why don't we play hookey and go for lunch, my treat."

"Don't mind if I do," Tessa said. Things were looking better already.

Devil Wind

The wind died with a soft sigh as though it were tired. Tony lifted his head cautiously from the steering wheel of his car. His eyes were hazy as he tried to focus.

Clarity finally took over and, shaking his head gently he was able to see through the windshield, except that it wasn't there!

There was devastation everywhere and his car was facing the wrong way. A large tree branch was in the back seat with the bent and buckled metal of the roof.

His only memory was the dark, roiling clouds that had gathered and followed him as he drove to visit his ailing mother. The silence now was deafening compared to the screeching wind that had formed the deadly tornado column.

He remembered trying to accelerate to get away from the sound, but it was too late to outrun the whirling wind. He didn't even know how long he'd been knocked out.

His senses gradually came back to him as he sniffed the air and thought he was hallucinating ... COFFEE? Tony looked around expecting to find an angel or someone.

The smell was very real. He remembered then, he never took a long journey without his life-saving coffee. Had the thermos survived? Reaching down on the passenger side he found it lying on its side, slowly leaking onto the floor. Grabbing it quickly, he lifted it and unscrewed the cracked cup. There was still some left. The most wonderful cup of coffee he'd tasted in his life!

DOUG GAYNOR - I

The Eraser

"Kill him! Kill him!"
"Get him! Get him!"
"Don't let him escape!"

I get more excited than most and jump up and down and yell all the time. There is no greater high than to see handsome muscular men battle each other at a wrestling match. I am a great fan and attend all the matches.

That's why I'm here tonight watching The Eraser meet Mad Dog Schultz for the championship. The winner receives the Golden Champion's belt of the World Federation. The arena is jammed packed with the beautiful people near the ring and the rest higher up. Needless to say, I am higher up. There is yelling and screaming everywhere adding to the noise of the grunting and slamming going on in the ring.

"Come on Schultzy! Get him!" the fat man two rows down shouts.

"Erase him! Erase him!" I yell to get back at the fat man.

The match continues on with both wrestlers evenly matched. The Eraser's favourite move used to be the Piledriver, but it has been banned after some wrestlers were permanently injured or died in the ring. Now he uses the Dropkick to knock his opponent down and then pins him after the Chokehold renders him unconscious. There he goes.

"Way to go, Eraser!"

The referee holds up the Eraser's hand and shouts, "The winner and champion is The Eraser."

The crowd goes wild and there is loud clapping and screaming. As the building empties, I hope to obtain his autograph and talk to him about a personal matter. Luckily, I made an arrangement with his manager beforehand.

As I walked down the stairs and entered the long corridor, my heart pounded with anxiety. The dressing room was at the end of the corridor and I knocked on the door.

The door opened and there stood before me a six foot seven, 275 pound hunk of a man. He smiled and motioned me to come in and sit down.

"My name is Linda Stark and your manager made arrangements for me to obtain your autograph."

"Oh yea. Do you have a program I can sign?"

"Here it is and I want to talk to you about something else. I understand that you have a business on the side called The Eraser Inc."

"Who told you about that? We don't advertise."

"A friend of mine told me. He used your service."

"Yes that's true. I do have a company. We erase or fix things. We erase graffiti from buildings, we clear up vacant lots and pursue the perpetrators. We help erase overdue accounts for companies and evict people from their premises, if necessary. We are involved in all kinds of situations. I make more money from my business than I do from wrestling. What can I do for you?"

"Well, I want to erase my husband. He abuses me physically and mentally and is very possessive."

"We are involved in a lot of areas but this request is a first for us, but not beyond possibility."

"What will it take to convince you?"

"It will be expensive. It will cost twenty-five thousand dollars with seventy-five per cent up front, all cash."

"I can raise the money in a couple of days and bring it to you."

"Good, it's a deal. I will complete the operation personally in about a week and remember you can't tell anybody about this. They don't call me The Eraser for nothing."

It's been two days since I delivered the cash and nothing has happened yet. I can't take anymore from Lou. He yells and insults me. Verbal abuse is worse than physical abuse. At least when he's gone, I can collect on the insurance. That's some consolation.

"Linda, where's my breakfast? Get a load of this on the sports page. It says The Eraser has been erased in a drive-by shooting. There goes your big hero, ha! ha!"

There goes my 18,000 dollars with nothing to show for it. What now? Maybe I should go the poisoning route or maybe I should make an appointment with Mad Dog Schultz.

DOUG GAYNOR - II

Kandahar

It's been eight months since deployment and I really miss him. Betsy and Allan keep asking me when Daddy is coming home? All I can answer is 'soon'. I don't want them to be alarmed over the absence of their father and feel all my pent up anxiety over what may happen. Being in the Army, we have lived overseas and across the country but have never had to endure a war situation. He calls me sparingly if conditions are right. Most of our contact is by letter, although I haven't received one lately. It's time to write him another one today.

•••••

My dearest Jimmy:

Are you all right? I haven't heard from you for some time. How is the situation around Kandahar? In your last letter, you mentioned that you were involved in training the Afghans in foot patrols. They should have been ready to take over from you by now. The last time I saw you, your hand was in the air waving goodbye when you left on the plane. I kept praying it wasn't the last goodbye. I tried to lead a normal life, but there is nothing normal about it. You are constantly on my mind.

Betsy and Allan miss you very much and I miss you most of all. I pray each day that you will be kept safe and return to us. Attached are a few drawings that the children did for you at school.

I know it's difficult to write but please, please try. I love you.

Laura

•••••

I haven't heard from him. The Army has been no help. Every time I try to obtain some information, the only answer I receive is that it's classified. The mail is slow but you'd think by now I would have heard something, a phone call or a letter. They say no news is good news and I have to keep up my hope. Without Betsy and Allan, I would be going out of my mind. I have to write again.

•••••

Jim honey:

I know I haven't had an letter or phone call from you but I just feel in my bones that you are all right. Betsy and Allan miss their daddy and they pray for you every night before going to bed. I saw on TV that the Taliban attacked a convoy in Kandahar. I hope you weren't anywhere near it. Your tour of duty is finally over next month and I am counting the days till you return. We will have a great homecoming for you. I love you.

Laura

•••••

The month passed and notification came to me that the unit was returning tomorrow at 2 o'clock. I couldn't sleep all night and time passed slowly. We hopped into the car the next day and headed to the airport. We parked and joined the crowd waiting the return of their loved ones.

"Look Mommy, I see the plane."

"I see it Betsy. Daddy will soon be here."

The plane banked to the right, descended and landed on the runway. It then taxied slowly on to the tarmac and powered down.

The ramp was pushed in to place. The door opened and smiling soldiers began to disembark. Families rushed forward to embrace their loved ones. Then the line of soldiers ended.

"Where's Daddy?"

"I don't know, Allan. I don't know," I replied, as fear swelled up within me. He's not here. Maybe he's dead! I started to cry.

"Wait Mommy, some more are coming, carrying a stretcher."

"It's Daddy, but he has no arms and legs."

"Oh my God, Oh my God," I cried, as I rushed towards Jimmy.

"I'm so sorry Laura, I'm so sorry. I'm a mess. A roadside bomb blew up on me."

"Jimmy, Jimmy, we'll work things out no matter how long. The main thing is that you are back with us again."

DOUG GAYNOR - III

Yakkety! Yak!

I'm cherishing every moment of my freedom. My children are all grown up, moved out and have a life of their own.

It's not that I don't miss them, but I have more time to spend with my wife, June, and to make plans according to our own agenda. We travel, go to parties and visit friends. It is very enjoyable.

One day, June came to me and said, "You know Dave, Mom is having a tough time on her own. She was able to cope since Dad died five years ago but now she has a hard time walking and needs some care."

"Well, she's not getting any younger."

"I've invited her to move in with us. We have lots of space and we can't afford to place her in a retirement home."

"What? Why didn't you check with me first? We no sooner have the place to ourselves and we have to start all over again."

"But she has nowhere to go. We can't leave her out on the

street. And she has nowhere else to go and I love her."

"Damn! I don't like it. I don't want to listen to that yakkety yak all the time. The woman never shuts up. She's so mouthy."

"Don't be cruel, Dave. Mom is a good woman."

"I know. When did you say she could come?"

"I said she could move in next week."

"So soon?"

"Yes. She could bring some of her furniture and use one of the girls' former bedrooms. We still have a few things to settle regarding the house, though."

"Damn! Okay, we'll give it a try." Mom moved in soon.

"Dave, thank you so much for letting me stay here. Some of my furniture will be arriving in a few days. How are the girls? I bet they are well. They were always pretty smart. How do you occupy your time now that you are retired? I guess you are pretty busy doing all the things you wanted to do. Do you still play bridge? Maybe, we can have a game sometime."

"Mother, your room is on the ground floor and is very convenient to everything."

"June, what's the matter with Dave? He seems to be in a grumpy mood all the time. I've been here eight months now and he never seems to talk much. I really appreciate you helping me, dear, and hope I haven't been too much trouble. My supply of Depends is nearly finished. Do you think Dave can get me some more?"

"Don't mind Dave. He gets moody sometimes. I'll send him to the store right away."

"Dave, do you think you can paint my room? I don't know what color yet, maybe a light brown or peachy color. I like tho se colors the best. They remind me of my own home where George and I lived for all those years. He used water based paint because the rollers and brushes were easy to clean. Do you use water based paint, Dave? If you don't, you should. How long do you think it would take to paint the whole room? I could sleep in the other room while you are painting my room."

"Well, mother, we should be able to paint it."

"June, does Dave barbecue anymore? He used to barbecue a lot, didn't he. Oh, there's Dave. Do you still barbecue?"

"I barbecue all the time."

"I love barbecue steaks, especially t-bone. I like to suck on the bone. George used to grill them. They need to be slightly marbled, seared first to seal in the juices and then cooked six minutes on each side. Baked potato and mushrooms should be a must also. Of course, the vegetables are cooked in foil. We ate outside on the patio close to nature and in the warm breezes. We sat under the umbrella as too much sun is not healthy."

"Do you read much, Dave? I used to read many books. My eyesight is not good now and I don't read as much. I really like Maeve Binchy and have read all her books. What kind of books do you read? I bet you prefer detective stories. All the men like them, trying to guess who did it. I like magazines too, especially Good Housekeeping. The recipes are excellent and I like to cook. I don't cook often now but I once won a prize for my cake. It was chocolate cake with chocolate icing."

"I only read the newspaper."

"I'm telling you, June, it's been two years and I can't stand it anymore. It's yakkety yak, yakkety yak all day long, seven days a week. It's driving me crazy."

"Calm down, Dave. Why don't you bring Mom her tea?"

"Okay, I will. I have to go upstairs for a minute."

Ah! There it is, in the bottom of the drawer, my magic ring with the fake stone that opens up. I used to perform magic tricks with it when the children were small. I'll go to the garage to put it to good use.

"I'll bring the tea now."

I opened the ring and mixed the contents into the tea.

The next day, Mother died. June was very upset and cried. Peace at last!!

MARY SANDOR - I

Forever Remembered...

I live alone now, often spending my solitary days with only my memories for company.

The memories. Some of them as alive in my heart as they were over 50 years ago. In my mind, the past is re-lived over and over again. At times I feel that if I reach out my arms, I can touch it, embrace it...

•••••

The afternoon sun gave the blue Mediterranean a jewel-like appearance as the golden rays sparkled on its surface. At the front of our ship, hundreds of dolphins were dancing in the azure waters, jumping up from the sea, playfully twisting their glistening, pearl coloured bodies toward the blue sky, then gliding back into the depths in unison, again and again, reminders of the Can-Can dancers from the stages of the long-ago Orpheum theatres.

We were standing on the top deck, near the bow of the ship, an Italian ocean liner, named Vulcania, just the two of us, Charles and I, amazed by this fantastic entertainment. The Vulcania was now clearing the Straits of Gibraltar, leaving behind the shores of Europe and Africa. Then our horizons widened as it welcomed the waters of the vast Atlantic Ocean.

We were going to Canada in pursuit of a new life, a life which promised liberty, freedom and democracy. A life that promised achievements, the attainment of growth and rewards for our future.

I tried to fill my heart with the joy of such expectancy, but from somewhere, from the deepest depth of my soul, the unbreakable ties of my past kept calling me back. "Come back," said my mother's tear-soaked face; "Come home," begged my father's pain-filled eyes.

"Go back, go home," said everything inside of me, as I listened to the perceived voices and images of my past. The green hills of Hûvösvölgy, the quiet streets of Zuglo, the turquoise coloured waters of Lake Balaton, and my ink-stained classroom in Budapest I graduated from not long ago, they were all with me on the deck of that ship, crying, demanding and begging.

But, something else surfaced in my heart. The sound of sirens, signalling the arrival of enemy aircraft, the horrors of the Second World War, then the remembrance of the tremendous fear and desperation as we lived under the oppression of a foreign political power, and the fearsome dictatorship of communism.

My mind saw the blood of innocents marring the sidewalks of Budapest during the recent Revolution of 1956; I heard the heart-ripping screams of parents finding their children dead on the streets or wounded by enemy fire. They were the teenagers and other youth, named "the Freedom fighters" of 1956, mere children often, but ready to die for the liberation of their homeland. I saw the fall of that sacred Revolution, and heard the desperate plight of my countrymen as they sought the help of the Free World, which never came, and finally their capitulation into the returning communist power.

And so we flee, along with many thousands of others. We flee in the hope of finding a better life, of finding peace and a future without fear, dogma and life-threatening inquisitions.

Charles and I left Hungary together, as an engaged couple. In January of 1957, prior to our immigration to Canada, we were married in a small ceremony in Maria Enzersdorf, a small town on the outskirts of Vienna. I loved him with all of my heart, and I wanted a future with him, and I wanted a safe, independent, war-free country to live in, where we could raise our children with dignity and assure them of a good life.

I knew I didn't want to turn back. I knew I wanted to stay at the side of this young man and share my life with him. However, I also knew that I will never forget my homeland, my family, my friends and my beloved city, Budapest. They will always be in my heart, loved and forever remembered.

I can attest to the fact that crossing the Atlantic in February is not much fun. The Vulcania fought storm after storm. Greyness and fog enveloped our ship, and the towering waves played with it as if the huge ocean liner was only a toy.

The crossing to Canada required 5 days. Almost every passenger was seasick. The open-air decks were closed to everyone, for the monstrous waves washed over them and spewed across them with lightning speed, powerfully sweeping everything in their way into the swirling depths. They were like demons from the sea unleashed. Once, through the portholes of our ship we saw something - quite far from us - looking like a ball being bounced up and down on top of that angry sea. Later we heard from the staff that it was also a ship, a passenger liner called the Arosa Star, sailing from Bremerhaven to Canada.

Being witness to the voyage of the Arosa Star held a deep significance for me, for a few months later this was the boat that brought my mother to Canada. She also escaped from Hungary and with the help of the Red Cross, found us.

On the 13th of February, 1957, the Vulcania arrived in Halifax, a major seaport in the province of Nova Scotia, Canada.

We did not see much of the city, for following our arrival we spent several hours in the port building, where the Canadian immigration officials interviewed us, the arriving passengers from the Vulcania, and declared us 'landed immigrants' to Canada.

I stood inside that building that looked no different from an old, dilapidated warehouse. Its walls and ceiling was of aged, dark wood, and musty air hung everywhere. The noise was deafening, for all the new arrivals seemed to speak all at once, everyone in their own language, and above all this, the loudspeakers carried constant messages of welcome and instructions, creating what seemed like the new biblical Babel. Sandwiches were passed around. The bread looked and tasted like it was made from white cotton. I tried to swallow some of it but my throat was constricted by the tears I tried to hold back.

Dear God, what are we doing here?

Following our officiating as landed immigrants to Canada, we, the refugees from Hungary, were escorted out of the building and onto a waiting train. With the help of an interpreter, we found out that we were to be taken to Vancouver, over 6000 kilometres from Halifax, a city on the shores of the Pacific Ocean, in the Canadian province of British Columbia.

Our train travel across the country was amazing and unbelievably beautiful. Following the colourful small towns of the East, we travelled through the frozen land of Northern Ontario, with its myriad lakes and rocks, framed by thousands of tall pines. The ground was covered by pristine snow, like a giant blanket, burying everything that held life; for we saw no habitation anywhere, save for a few parka-and-hood-covered rail workers here and there on the rail line, and once in a while an odd car, travelling parallel with our train on the shimmering, icy roadway.

Leaving the province of Ontario, we travelled through the prairies of Manitoba and Saskatchewan, which, in winter time was also snow-covered, but dotted with picturesque farms and silos.

The sight of the Rocky Mountains of Alberta and British Columbia filled us with awe. We spent almost all of our time in the scenic observation car of the train, enjoying the fantastic sight of the towering, snow-capped mountains, the ancient glaciers and the serene beauty of the turquoise mountain lakes. We saw luxurious ski resorts, chalets, ski lifts and skiers and the vacationers of this stylish winter-sports paradise.

Our accommodations on this train - called the "Transcontinental" – were excellent. We slept in bunk beds in private quarters, ate great food served on fine china, accompanied by gleaming silver cutlery, in an amazing, art-deco styled dining car.

But we all knew that the most important task for us was to learn the English language, so my husband and I decided to learn a hundred words per day, and we did. By the time, we arrived at our destination, we took pride in having five hundred English words in our vocabulary.

All of the new Hungarian immigrants were taken off the train at the town of Chilliwack, about a hundred kilometres east of the city of Vancouver, and bussed to another town named Abbotsford, where accommodations were waiting for us in the local military barracks.

Men and women were housed in separate quarters, and food was provided by the military's kitchen staff.

Some weeks later, buses came again, sent by Canadian Immigration officials from Vancouver, and we were told that some of us would be taken to Vancouver, where jobs were waiting for us. Charles and I were selected along with others, and so with much enthusiasm we left for our final destination on this long journey, to finally start our new life in our adopted country.

On arrival in Vancouver, this beautiful city by the Pacific (dear God, how far is this from Budapest?), we were told by the local immigration officials that some mistakes had been made, for there were no jobs for any of us just then. However, they did not send us back to Abbotsford, but housed us, for lack of other accommodations, in their in-house jail cells.

We spent some rather boring and sad days, locked in those cells, Charles and I again separated from each other. We were able to leave our cells whenever we wanted to, but were locked up again when we returned.

A few days later, my husband and I were told that a Canadian family had been found for us in Vancouver, with whom we would be staying until we found jobs for ourselves.

For our room and board, the Immigration Office paid 40 dollars monthly to this family.

Our landlady was also an immigrant to Canada, with two young daughters. We never met her husband, for he was away in Northern British Columbia, at a logging camp. We worked for our keep, cleaned the house, did the laundry and the dishes, looked after the girls; my husband cut the grass and weeded the garden, washed windows and painted the outside of the house, on request from our hostess. All this for our keep, for we never received monetary compensation for our labour. I didn't cook much during the week, for the food was made and rationed by our landlady. Dinner six days a week consisted of a bowl of Campbell's tomato soup, poured out from a can, to which some, also canned, condensed Carnation milk was added. Beside the soup, we got a sandwich, made with the white cotton bread.

I must say, we were amazed that our landlady and her daughters lived on that too and it was enough for them. On Sundays though, we all had roast beef, the same every Sunday - while we lived there.

Before long, we were working. Charles was hired as a building construction worker, wheel barrelling concrete on the floors of the unfinished high-rises. I was terrified for him, afraid he may fall, or hurt himself some way, for he had never worked in this manner; he was a drafting designer in Hungary.

My first job in Vancouver was at the local bus depot, cleaning the insides of the long distance Greyhound buses. Later, I washed dishes in a restaurant. We had to take these positions, for we did not speak the English language properly, and were, therefore, not qualified for the better jobs.

Our first home was a one room "walk-up to the top floor" in a private, three story house. We were happy to be on our own, and quite enthused about starting our new life in Canada. Still, the nicest moment of our day was when we sat down at our rickety, old, rented table and wrote letters home, telling our loved ones about our good fortune, and the joys of our daily lives. We never wrote about the hardships, for we did not want them to worry about us.

It often rains in Vancouver. We spent many rainy days in that third floor room, right under the roof, hearing the quiet rain knocking on top, while listening to the sound of fog horns from the bay. They were there to warn the ships moving in the harbour, as the constant fog of the fall months enveloped the bay.

Oh, how I didn't want to be here! I wanted to be home, walking in the early autumn sunshine, yes, somewhere in Buda, right under those large oak trees, with the sun shining through the yellowing leaves, bathing me in golden warmth. I wanted to walk the streets I knew so well since childhood. I wanted to see my friends and family. I wanted to go home to my old house in Budapest and I wanted to hug all doors and windows and the walls surrounding my beloved home.

Then we heard the news. On June 16, 1958. They hanged Imre Nagy and Pál Maléter, along with other leaders of the anti-Soviet revolution. Dear God, where were you then?

Then the message came from home:

"Members of the AVH (the Hungarian Secret Police) took grandfather away in the middle of the night. They came for him in a canvas-covered truck. We don't know where he is. We don't know where they took him and why. Did he say something against the regime? Did someone overhear and report him?"

I had nightmares again, just like back at home during and after the Revolution. Often, I woke up screaming, thinking that I heard the screeching sound of metal from the Soviet tanks returning to Budapest.

I realised I was very lucky washing dishes in a Canadian restaurant.

It was not easy to start a new life in a foreign land, without language skills, monetary resources or employable experience. But whatever hardships we faced, we faced them together, my husband and I. I knew he was always there for me, loving me, helping me. Together we built a home and raised our children.

We learned the English language and acquired skills which gave us better opportunities in obtaining more valued employment. Our appreciation and love for our adopted country matured and deepened. Our lives were spent here for the most part in happiness and contentment.

My homeland will always be in my heart, I will always love the land where I was born, where my cradle rocked.

But there is another land, a small parcel of land only, inside a nicely kept cemetery on a hill, overlooking the town of Bolton, in Ontario. There, under an old, aged maple tree rest the earthly remains of my mother and father. Not long ago, we buried my husband beside them. His headstone carries my name also, awaiting the date of my death to be carved into it.

As I stand above the graves, a sense of belonging fills my heart.

I know this is where I want to be; this is where I want to be laid to rest, next to my loved ones. Until then I want to live here, amid the loving circle of my children and grandchildren.

Still, during many quiet and lonely nights as my heart re-visits the land of my youth, my eyes fill with tears, as my soul yearns for that faraway place in my memories.

MARY SANDOR - II

The Seasons

I will never forget the first time I saw Spring. She was youth and beauty, vibrant with the scent of apple blossoms and lilac trees. I fell for her charms, her blossoming gardens and her fields of wildflowers. I danced in her green meadows to the harmonious tunes of her songbirds, and waded into her clear and shallow streams. I lay on her silky new grass and looked above me at the bright blue skies she offered. She gave me renewed energy and joy, and I wanted her to be mine forever.

Then I met Summer. Wild, hot Summer. She bedazzled me. The moment I saw her, I knew I loved her with all the passion I possessed. She offered me her world and I wanted it. I wanted her glorious, sun-filled days and her sensuous, intoxicating nights. I wanted her promenade of colourful flowers and her garden scents. I wanted to bask in her glorious light, letting her heat envelope my heart and take me to each new day.

Until Autumn came into my life. She carried within her a tranquil maturity. When I looked at her, all I could see was colours, hues of all kinds that graced her beauty. Her sunshine did not burn me, but gave me warmth. She turned my passion into gentle joy and the appreciation for the changing scenes of life. I wanted to be with her for as long as I could, to celebrate my life and look back on my memories.

Then one day she was gone. Her trees were barren, the dead leaves scattered on the ground and she herself was encrusted in frost.

And I encountered Winter. She was also beautiful, and while she had my admiration, I could never love her frozen beauty. Her world was pristine, but colourless.

A white blanket of snow covered everything she created. Her harsh winds were fearsome and her fury generated blinding storms. I hid from her cajoling whisper: "Come, let's play. Let's build ice castles and make snowmen, let's go skate and ski. Let's have fun in my snow."

No, I could not, for I feared her; I wanted her gone. And soon the old year turned into new, and one day the Sun smiled upon her, making her mellow and mild. She lost her rigid power and as she melted into oblivion, she whispered to me once more: "Never mind my demise. Look ahead instead. You see, Spring is coming back, she is just around the corner."

MARY SANDOR - III

Remember

Remember our laughter;
Not our tears.
Remember our joys;
Not our fears.

> Remember us young;
> Working and sharing.
> Remember us loving;
> And always caring.

Remember our walks
In the quiet rain;
Those glorious summers,
That sparkling lake.

> Remember the garden;
> The flowering trees,
> The scent of the blooms,
> The hum of the bees.

Remember the children;
The blessings, the joys,
The warm little hands
Holding onto yours.

> Remember our love,
> Untouched by age;
> The oath and the pledge,
> The promises we made

Remember that ever
I'll be by your side;
In sickness and in health,
Forever, your wife!

RENA FLANNIGAN - I

Dreamy Wishes

I have your picture before me each and every day, you are my constant companion. You know nothing of this, of course. How could you? You scarcely knew me. Yes, we met, a long time ago, and I remembered you, but doubt that you even gave me another thought after our meeting.

I am alone a lot, so I talk to you. I ask you about things and get no answers. I tell you things and ask your advice; again, I get no answer, but I feel that it is nice to be able to 'get things off my chest'. Sometimes, I feel better for talking to you, thank you for being there.

We met at a gathering of mutual friends and when I saw you my heart did a flip. I thought how much I would like to get to know you. Our hostess introduced us and we chatted for a while. In our short conversation, I discovered we had a lot in common and that does not happen often in my life.

Things I am interested in don't seem to be of interest to the majority of people I know, so it was exciting to think that this stranger and I did share ideas. Others listen but escape as quickly as they can; they stay long enough in my company to be polite and then make excuses to leave.

A normal happening when I try to make or join a conversation is to be cut-off in the middle of a sentence, as if I had not even been talking at all. I don't like it but I have to accept that I must be a bit of an odd character – no, you are not an odd character, you were really nice, and I enjoyed listening to you when you spoke – which is why it was so nice to find another human being who shared my interests. I am so tempted to say to the other person, "Excuse me, I was not finished what I was saying." On rare occasions, I do say that but mostly I don't say anything.

I get the message that what I am telling them is of no interest or boring to them so I leave it alone. I never want to cause any waves within the company and I know it would make the other person feel bad, embarrassed or angry although they were the cause of it. I would find it very embarrassing to myself to do that, so I say nothing. They are the ones who are rude in my estimation and they are not worth getting upset about.

When I talk to you I can talk a blue streak; I know you will listen – as if you have a choice. If I feel down you are there, if I feel happy I love to share the happiness with you. I tell you about my family and how each of them is progressing; how the baby is so brilliant, naturally, she is after all my great granddaughter, isn't she? I tell you all she does and is learning daily. She is into everything; she is so adventurous.

I tell you too about our other baby, my niece's little girl. She is so pretty and has the most gorgeous blue eyes; her hair is a mass of beautiful blonde curls. When she smiles, she has beautiful dimples. The two babies are such a joy to have around and they love each other; when they see each other first thing in the morning they become so excited. The one runs around and the other crawls at a rate of about a mile a minute trying to keep up.

Even when I feel in the mood for someone to share loving thoughts, you are there. I like that very much. I look into your eyes in the photo and think what amazing brown eyes you have; they seem almost liquid to gaze into.

Sometimes, it is as if you have a devil's twinkle in them and other times it is as if you are contemplating things deeply. I look at the shape of your mouth in the photo and think; if you were a woman, your smile would be as enigmatic as Mona Lisa's. Are you smiling a sweet smile, are you smiling with a hidden meaning, or are you laughing at me? I will never know the answer; it is in how I see you at the time. I do know that I love you for being there. I remembered you have a great sense of humour. Is that why you smile as you do?

I wish often that you were real and a part of my life, but at the same time if you were there, would these lovely thoughts survive? Would the meeting make me realise I am only fantasizing? Is it true that absence makes the heart grow fonder? I know my heart certainly has grown very fond of you. One thing though, out of sight out of mind can never enter my imagination.

Being only a part of my dreams, we will never argue about anything. On the other hand, if we did have a disagreement it would be lovely making up again. I do not want to take a chance either way; I want to love you as you are then we will always be happy together. I know it is not realistic, but this is my dream and I can imagine only nice things in it if I want to. I do so want to!.

When I go to bed at night, I kiss your photo and wish you good night. I imagine you coming to my bed and making love with me. That won't happen either but it is a pleasant thought. I can feel your loving arms enfold me to keep me safe, should I have a bad dream; you will comfort me so tenderly. I know you will.

After all, in my dream, you are a perfect lover who cares that I have a satisfying experience every bit as much as you did. If only! Naturally, you will have marvellous hugs for me, you will rub my back and I will curl up in your arms and fall asleep. We will of course, fit to each other like pieces of a jigsaw puzzle. Is that not a wonderful thought? I like it. Yes my love, I will do everything I can to make these experiences as good for you as you will for me. We are lovers; I am not a taker without any thought for your feelings.

After imagining a beautiful night together, it will eventually be time to face a new day. When I awake I will reach for you beside me and be sad that I was only dreaming that you had been there. I will lie in half-sleep, wake slowly and fantasize again about the emotions of the night before.

I am consoled knowing that I can have you with me when once again night falls and it is time to retire. In my dream we kiss good morning, we might even make love again or just lie with our arms entwined in a gorgeous hug. Then you will insist on getting up to make coffee and will bring one to me.

While we are sitting in bed drinking our coffee, we will chat about what we will do for the rest of the day. You see darling, we will always be together and life will be so different for me so long as I have your photo to talk to.

Far from reality, I will hold you in my dream until my last breath. Facing the grim day-to-day events will never enter our life together. When I met you, you unknowingly brought joy into my life and I will always be grateful that you did. I am only sorry I never had the chance to share such happiness with you in reality. I hope that your life has been happy, albeit not with me but with someone else. I like to think that somewhere in your memory I might have popped into your memory of the evening we met. I am so pleased I had a chance to take a photo of you that night to be able to share my thoughts and feelings with. I love you.

Take care my love, know that I will be yours and you mine forever – in my dreams.

RENA FLANNIGAN - II

A Mistake With No Regrets!

My mentor Jeanette was ill, so we did not have our usual little silk bag to draw a subject from. So it was suggested we do a story about an "odd character" or "our biggest mistake". It is now Tuesday night and I am at wondering what to write this week. Not because I don't know, or have not met, some odd characters in my time. There have been a few of them along the way. As for making mistakes, who hasn't, but which ones do we want to admit to?

I would have to say that my mistakes had to do with Mexico! The first time I ever visited Puerto Vallarta and saw the fascinating Sierra Madre Mountains surrounding the small, typically old Mexican town, I declared, "I love it" and we know a woman in love can make some bloopers. Boy, did I make a few of them. Not everything was a mistake though. In 1983, I went there on holiday with my mother who was not well at the time, and who was always cold. I wanted to get her to somewhere warm. It was warm, believe me! We left a very cold December in Toronto and landed in 75 F. Mum loved it!

Everywhere we turned, there were Timeshare sales people inviting us to presentations to many hotels with timeshare facilities. Managing to resist these, but interested in knowing more about them, I found myself one day at a hotel which had a championship tennis club attached to it. At that time I played quite a bit of tennis, so I approached a salesman and asked to have the concept explained to me. He showed me around and I loved the view from one unit right on the ocean and beach. Do I have to tell you – I bought it! It was too bad that my time in this unit finished after 25 years of my own little slice of Paradise and luxury.

Now starts the beginning of the "error of my ways"! One week was not enough so when I had the chance to buy a second week I did so, this time I bought a 2-bedroom unit hoping my family would eventually be able to join me there. We all loved the place and the people at the hotel. The only problem was money, as it usually is, for the family to afford to come south! Again a good move and if I had left it there that would have been fine but no, I had to try to do better by buying another unit in another hotel! Even this was not bad since I was able to use this one for trading power in several places of the world and certainly the price was right each time. So what was my mistake then?

Knowing the ropes very well by now, I should have left things alone but not me, no sir! Twice I found myself talking to sales people I thought I could trust. Who can trust a salesman? I still shake my head at my foolishness when I found myself signing away more and more dollars based on the promises of fellow countrymen who assured me they would not give me a run-around, that they would be able to sell off what I had in excess – liars! My intention was to try to sell one unit I had bought and knew I would never get the full use of, although I did hope that now my granddaughters were growing up and earning their own money, they might be able to use the remainder of whatever time was left. I think they will, they love the place as much as I do.

Not all mistakes are bad, fortunately. Yes, I made mistakes buying so much time but I have had many years of pleasure from most of these 'mistakes'. The girls are old enough to start doing the same, and finally my family have also been able to join me for the holidays. Many people don't like the concept of Timesharing. In its defence I have to say my mistakes have turned out to be about the best thing I ever did.

I have been able to stay in the heart of Vienna, twice in beautiful bungalow accommodation in Australia, a lovely lakeside lodge right here in Ontario and a favourite, one in Ireland, an old Abbey with creaky floors that was built in 1437. I must not forget when talking of luxury, the place three of us had the use of in Collingwood, only a drive of a couple of hours from home! Being in that one gave me a real sense of what the rich live like believe me.

It had two Jacuzzis to begin with and I cannot bend enough to be able to get into them. I run the water as deep as my ankles but realized there was no way I could get down to use it. Big tears of frustration on that front I assure you, I love the Jacuzzis. I even traded into the heart of Stratford on Avon where my granddaughter and I went to see one of the Bard's plays. Not forgetting the spa accommodation in Hungary, this time for three people.

I have to think 'where did I really make mistakes' in the end? They cost me a lot of money, true, but I had more than the value of the cost eventually. Hotel rooms are $150.00 and up for a night's sleep, I get accommodation for seven people for about $125.00 a night and we only unpack once. Eating is not a problem, we have cooking facilities and that cuts costs as well. All in all, I think these were the biggest and best 'mistakes' I ever made! I know that if I had not made my mistake I would maybe make it to Centre Island and, if I looked after my pennies, have an economy holiday every other year.

Some mistakes are good to make as far as I am concerned and I do not regret mine in this case.

RENA FLANNIGAN - III

The Wheels of Life Are Turning

From high chair to wheelchair,
Life has a beginning and an end.
With many highs and lows at every bend;
Some straight paths, some curves and hills.

> With Nature's sign a woman accepts
> With happy thoughts and with no fear.
> She knows a baby soon she'll bear;
> A mother to be has a premonition.

A baby comes in all due time;
It matters not if girl or boy.
A constant source of love and joy.
The babe is a blessing from above;

> Soon the child is fully-grown;
> School, teens, families of their own.
> As middle age appears, they're right in the middle;
> Suddenly, they have two sets of children.

Life's roles are now reversed.
A position no one ever rehearsed.
Parents become the "new" children;
They need the attention. My, how things change!

> Hurts from a fall, hearts broken on the way;
> The parents said wait, the pain will go away.
> Will all the love and care they gave,
> Be forgotten when needed most

The baby stroller had four wheels;
Four for a wheelchair too.
A beloved, and loving parent there,
Remember days gone by and give good care!

MARGARET CAREY - I

David *(Based on actual events)*

He rolled down the window of the car and took a deep breath. The warm September air filled his lungs with the smell of pine trees that lined the miles of highway. He was on his way home.

The weekend at his sister's cottage in the Thousand Islands was just what he needed to regroup and regenerate after that knock-down-drag-out fight he had with David on Friday.

They had met 15 months ago in a gay bar in Toronto. He remembered the day like it was yesterday. He spotted David right away standing by the bar, chatting with a tall muscular blond guy. It was hard not to notice him; tall with jet black hair and those piercing amethyst blue eyes, he was the perfect front page of GQ magazine. Summoning up his courage, he walked up and introduced himself to the two men, a risky move at best, but it paid off. David smiled and invited him to have a drink with them. The big blond guy just snarled and walked away.

They spent the evening together and ended up at David's apartment on Wellesley Street in the heart of downtown. The sex was incredible. David was a skilled, considerate yet insatiable lover, and that night they fell asleep exhausted and entwined in each other's arms.

Shortly afterwards, he moved into David's Wellesley Street

apartment and they began the daily life as a couple in a city which was slowly accepting the emergence of the gay community as a separate and powerful entity. After all, it was 1984!

Their life hummed along like any other city life, full of its challenges, its ups and its downs. The only drawback was David's extraordinary good looks which constantly attracted both male and female attention. And David did not discourage it. In fact, he sometimes sought it. And that was what caused the escalating disagreement on that Friday night in September when, frustrated and angry, he slammed the door of the apartment with the words "I'm outta here!"

He called his sister from a phone booth outside to ask her if he could visit for a while.

Now he was on his way back. Back to the place he called his home. Back to the man who was his lover and his best friend. He tried to recall how the Friday argument began, but could not.

He laughed aloud realizing how we, as stupid human beings, could allow our emotions to ruin perfectly fixable moments in our lives. But he would fix that. He would buy a good bottle of wine on the way and apologize for the explosion. And that would be that. They would start again. They would find their way back to each other and to the vows they made together to live their lives in harmony and love.

He parked the car in the underground parking lot and walked - no, ran up the seven flights of stairs so not to waste any time waiting for the elevator.

Turning the key, he opened the door. The apartment was quiet. He noticed that the door of the coat closet was wide open and David's leather jacket was not there; he must have gone out. Oh well, he would wait with the wine and an apology.

The kitchen looked unusually messy. There were dirty dishes in the sink – totally out of character for the very tidy David. On the table he noticed two cups of unfinished coffee. He found this odd and slightly disturbing. Did David have company on the weekend?

He walked towards the bedroom. The door was closed and there was a brown smear on the doorknob. He stood for a moment trying to take all this in. This was so out of character with what he knew about his partner. And as he stood there, he noticed a strange smell. He could not place it. It was reminiscent of the smell of rust, or of wet iron.

He turned the doorknob and walked in.

For a few moments, he felt like he was in a dream. Nothing about this made any sense to him. The room was bathed in waning light which made the scene even more surreal. He never saw so much blood. Blood soaked the bed and dripped in rivulets onto the carpet where it lay in drying, rusty pools.

David lay naked and face down on the bed with his arms out-stretched. Each wrist was fastened by leather strap to the iron post of the bed's headboard. His black hair was matted with blood, and his neck, back and buttocks covered in numerous slashes, barely visible under the smears and pools of clotting, drying blood. The handle of the kitchen knife buried in his back loomed ominously from under his left shoulder blade.

He stood transfixed by the horror, still not processing the full extent of the scene, unable to move, unable to make a sound for fear of waking himself up from this nightmare, yet knowing that this was terribly real.

As senses returned to their normal function, his knees buckled and he vomited on the floor.

Slowly, he crawled out of the bedroom, picked up the telephone and called 911.

MARGARET CAREY - II

El Diablo

It was a perfect Cuban day when we arrived on the uninhabited island of Cayo Blanco via an old Russian Kamov helicopter. The flight was at best precarious, as there were no doors on the wretched thing and seatbelts were obviously not invented at the time of its creation. As we slid along its slippery benches, we watched the land below in horror and clutched the bars above for dear life.

In the end, it was all worth it as the snorkelling in the clear azure sea proved to be outstanding, and the beach was powdery and white as icing sugar.

Lunch was served in the forested area of the island on something that resembled picnic tables. The food was delicious and we ate ravenously, washing it down with glasses of really bad Cuban wine which went down surprisingly easy; possibly due to the inhalation therapy of incredible sea air and the scent of pine mixed with smoke from the primitive barbeque.

Residual terror from the helicopter ride and subsequent joy at having survived it mixed with the appetite accelerator obtained through snorkelling made the repast even more delightful.

The next adventure was to be a horseback ride in the forest.

There were five of us who signed up for this excursion and we eagerly anticipated the arrival of the cavalry. At last five somewhat apathetic horses were led into the clearing where we waited. This made me ponder the moniker of "uninhabited" as given to the island, and I was pretty sure that the horses did not arrive on the helicopter with us.

Since I had ridden quite a bit in the past, the last thing I wanted is to plod along at a snail's pace while my not so comfortable in the saddle compatriots struggled to remain on top and not on the side or, oh horror , on the underside of their horses.

So I sidled up slyly to the old guide, who was in the process of assigning each horse to its rider, and pushing a five dollar note into his grizzled hands whispered, "Bueno caballo, por favor."

That was all the Spanish I knew other than ¿cuánto cuesta? and ¿Dónde está el baño?, and I hoped that he would understand that I wanted a good horse and not him.

He sized me up for a moment and disappeared into the woods only to reappear momentarily leading a jet black horse that danced and pranced like Pavlova on amphetamines. He handed me the reins and quietly said, "El Diablo."

Oh crap. My life flashed before my eyes. What did I get myself into? Now, I had Satan himself to ride. Served me right.

I mounted this monstrosity wondering if I bit off more than I could chew, but El Diablo stood patiently and neighed quietly in approval. Secure on the back of my fiery steed I sat and waited for the rest of the crew to be ready for our walk.

And waited...

And waited...

The old Cuban came up to me and pointed towards the small path which led into the forest.

"You go," he said in perfectly bad English.

"I go where?"

"You go," he said, a little less politely, pointing to the path.

The rest of the group was still figuring out which side of the horse to get up on, so the Cuban's directive was becoming very appealing. At this point, the old man decided that he used up all the energy on words and just waved me towards the woodland path.

Oh well, no guts, no glory... I turned Satan towards the path and nudged him gently. He responded quickly. Hmmm... This could really be a buen caballo, I thought.

Off we went. Slowly at first, and then seeing that the well-worn path seemed to go on and on, I squeezed El Diablo's side and clucked a universally recognized (by horses only) signal for 'let's get the heck out of here'.

And to my delight, that was what we did.

Trot turned to canter and then to a gallop. The group was left far behind and only the startled birds fluttered out of the trees as we flew by.

Suddenly, the path ended and what I saw took my breath away.

In front of us stretched miles and miles of untouched white beach and softly lapping waves of a turquoise sea. El Diablo snorted and lifted his head into the wind. He took a big breath in and I couldn't help but do the same. This was a picture from a novel, a painting of paradise and had there been a handsome man on a white stallion, every girl's dream.

I turned El Diablo to the right and we stood with our side to the ocean. Somehow he knew what I was going to ask him, because he snorted and pawed the wet sand waiting for my command.

I did not make him wait. I squeezed his sides and clucked softly. That was all he needed and we flew. The wind whipped through my hair and reddened my cheeks. El Diablo's hooves threw up a spray of salty water that glistened and shone with rainbow colours before it returned into the waiting arms of the sea. The beach seemed endless and as we galloped, lost in our own rapture, I swear I could see the sprouting of wings on the black shimmering back of my horse.

My dark Pegasus. How appropriate for my life.

I still think of my dark horse on those cold February days when aging bones ache with every humid day. All I have to do is close my eyes and we are flying once again, young and free with wind in our hair/mane, fans of sea spray landing on my thighs and El Diablo's joy, electric and palpable, mixing with mine as it travels back and forth through the reins.

MARGARET CAREY - III

When My Life's Lantern Is Extinguished

And when my life's lantern is extinguished, what will there be for me to do?

Perhaps I'll fly away to a magic land where aquamarine waters lap upon the golden sands of Everland.

There I will swim with dolphins and gossip with the mermaids among the coral castles of Atlantis.

Perhaps I'll dance among the treetops with the rogue wind that makes the leaves swoon at his sight, and chase the squirrel monkeys as they play.

Or maybe, in the darkest night I'll shimmer to the Aurora disco nights and, while chasing fireflies, watch as my wings become opalescent with a thousand glimmering lights.

I'll scoop up sands of the Sahara in my hand, and let them gently slide between my fingers, just like our life together slipped through pages of the calendar as we were planning our tomorrows.

Maybe I'll lie down with savannah lions in the shade of the acacia tree and watch the cubs wrestling the day away, or run with the wild horses, fingers entwined in the mane of the black stallion, my cheeks red with the wind and my immortal heart beating in rhythm with the hooves.

Perhaps I'll fly with the wild geese and watch the towns below that teem with life, like anthills somewhere on the edge of a forgotten forest.

Or I will float upon the lake, bathing in water and in moon glow, long after the loons have ceased their evening calls to prayer.

I'm certain that I will sleep upon your pillow, and leave
behind the faintest scent of perfume.

And you, upon the waking hour, will softly call my name
believing that I just left your bed.

And when I have cast off my earthly coat, no longer
needed in my flight, where shall I go?

Perhaps I'll float in on a moonbeam and gently kiss my
babies' cheeks as they, believing this a dream, smile
in their sleep letting the calm descend.

Or maybe I will make snow angels in your front yard in
the night, or sculpt icicles on eavestroughs to catch
the winter prism lights.

One thing I'm certain of; I will not lie beneath the
earth, and suffocating wait for visitors to bring me
flowers, and light small candles which, flickering for
a moment or two, will die upon my chest.

So celebrate my freedom. Please celebrate the lightness
of my being, for all too soon it will be time.

And then I'll show you all the places I discovered after I
cast off all those heavy robes of life.

JAN de GRIJS - I

Sandbanks Off Florida

On one of the outer islands in Southeast Florida, there existed a series of barren sand bars. The waters in this area were a toxic soup caused by effluent from industrial plants, intensive farming and the leak of deuterium from a nearby reactor.

Normal fauna and flora could not grow in this slop. No one really cared, though the Army Corps of Engineers did on rare occasions dredge the channel leading to a marina belonging to a developer who was going broke.

Life forms based on carbon chains failed to grow in this mess. A colony of microbes evolved using the toxic stew as a food source. These microbes were relatively large single cell organisms whose chemistry was based on silicon chains. As individuals, they lived happily chomping away at the abundant food supply devoid of competition from other organisms. At times they would meet and exchange thoughts for they were very smart.

Running along the seabed in the area, there was an array of data cables linking internet, government, NSA, industrial computers, servers and main frames.

The microbes as a unit managed to gain access to the data flowing through the cables and were startled by the stupidity of some of the users.

The intelligence of these microbes was based on pure mathematics. The microbes would correct software and add additional information obtained from sites such as Google and Wikipedia. If they needed information beyond their knowledge, they would scan the internet.

Some of the land-based users would get annoyed when software was rewritten, and blamed the Russians or Nigerians for mucking up their programmes. NSA was puzzled by frequent intrusions of their computer systems but later would blame Snowden. The microbes would chuckle at how dumb the users were. The toxic sludge community happily enjoyed life and were beginning to grow in significant numbers and solving many mathematical problems. They even won a prize in a mathematical competition, though the organizers never figured out where to send it.

On a cool fall day, a warning went out from the hurricane centre about an approaching category five storm. The microbes did not understand what the fuss was all about. They had not been around long enough to live through a storm surge. The winds increased in strength and turbid water swirled around.

The world of the microbes was starting to unravel as they were being buffeted about. The sand bar, which was their home, vanished into the North Atlantic. The life giving toxic stew washed away. No food resulted in the microbes dying of hunger.

In the aftermath of the storm, the Army Corps of Engineers redredged the channels and attempted to recreate the original landform. No one in the world was aware that an alternative life form had come into being, thrived for a brief period, and vanished. The computer programmers were sure their increased security had deterred hackers from messing up their programs.

JAN de GRIJS - II

The Bare Facts

We were eight kayakers into the third week of our trip in Northeast Greenland National Park. Today's campsite was on a sandy beach beneath a glacial boulder scarp. For the first time on the trip, the weather was sunny, warm and with no wind. The decision was made to spend the day hiking in the mountains.

After a leisurely breakfast, preparations were made for the day's hike; lunches prepared and daypacks packed.

"Bear," whispered Doug, as he pointed at the rim of the scarp. Seven pairs of eyes looked up at the rim where a polar bear sat staring down at us. Its coat yellow stained, black glistening nose and the black eyes were clearly visible to all.

"Where's the shotgun?" asked Lois.

"In the bottom of my kayak," replied Sally

"Who's got the shells?" asked Lois.

"I have them in my camera case," answered Doug.

Sally and Lois slowly edged over to where the kayaks were tethered. The shotgun lay in its scabbard in the water at the bottom of the kayak. The scabbard with the gun was retrieved and the water logged gun removed. Water dripped from its muzzle. Others in the group retrieved flares, bear bangers and shotgun shells. Sally loaded a flare into the shotgun. Doug looked around and realized Diana was missing. He spotted her beside a stream bathing. Doug shouted, "Bear!"

Diana stood up, unclad, with soapsuds in her hair, raised her arms, pirouetted, and said, "Yes, isn't it great. The first time in two weeks that I can bathe and wash my hair."

"Not that kind of bare. Bear as in polar bear."

"Oh," as she looked in the direction Doug was pointing. A long pause ensued. "What should I do?"

"Put some clothes on and come and join us." Diana began the task of dressing keeping an eye on the bear.

The rest of the group gathered together looking at the bear and wondering what it would do next. Suddenly, it stood up and sauntered down the scarp and approached the tents. The group now comprehended the bear's size using the tents as reference points.

"Shit, it's big," whispered Patty. Cameras clicked. Diana rejoined the group wearing damp clothes and flocks of suds on her hair. The bear closed in.

Sally raised the shotgun and pulled the trigger. Bang! A green flare arced through the air. "The bloody thing still works," muttered Sally peering at the gun in utter amazement.

The bear neared Patty's tent ignoring the flare as it passed over. It stopped at her tent, gave it a nip and it bounced back. Frustrated, the bear swatted the tent with its huge broad paw. "Hey, leave my tent alone," yelled Patty.

Flares and bear bangers were fired in rapid succession. The bear looked up as flares flashed overhead and was oblivious to the bangs around it. Later we encountered the Sierras Sledge Patrol personnel who told us polar bears are used to bangs and crashes created by the ice and the northern lights so what we did was of little use.

At this point Sally loaded slugs as the flares seemed not to be a deterrent. Doug was toying with a mangled bear banger, "I wonder if this thing still works?" He pulled the trigger; the banger fizzled through the air landing close to the bear.

Smoke billowed forth as the bear raised its head, sniffed the air, turned and sprinted away from the campsite. Nearing the shoreline, it lay down on some rocks and went to sleep. Everyone stood and gaped at the sleeping bear.

An animated discussion ensued and the outcome was to pack up and move away from this campsite. The gear was packed and the kayaks loaded with someone always on guard watching the bear. The kayaks were launched and as we departed. the bear raised it head and watched us for some time.

JAN de GRIJS - II

First Day Of Kayaking On The Zhupanova River

From the Karymsky Volcano base camp we spent three days hiking down to Camp Ruslan situated on the East Branch of the Zhupanova River.

Much of the first day was spent on traversing the flanks of the volcano. This involved river crossings, marching through swamps, then along river banks with ice covered sections which were steep and slippery. The following two days was all about crossing and re-crossing the river and bashing our way through alders. Late on the third day, we arrived at Camp Ruslan; it had rained the entire time we had been hiking. We were soggy, but a welcome fire awaited us. That afternoon and the next day was spent assembling kayaks. It continued to rain.

On the fifth day, we were ready to start kayaking down the Zhupanova River. The 'put in' spot was just above the junction of the East and West branches of the river. We had been instructed on how to handle the kayaks going down the river. "Use the ferry technique," said Olaf.

Then came the actual departure. We set off attempting to follow the given instructions, but upon reaching the spot where the two branches of the river met, we were cast into a maelstrom of fast running water. Techniques went out the window and just keeping some semblance of control became increasingly difficult. We ping-ponged from one bank to another. From time to time, we did regroup in a couple of eddies. Many tributaries increased the flow of water. Compounding the problem were numerous strainers along the river banks. Strainers consist of trees which have fallen into the river and the water is forced through the resulting debris. This can be dangerous to kayakers.

We were running through a swift section of the river, avoiding strainers, but ahead of us a tree in the water had trapped Charlotte and Tom. They were upside down. In a flash, I realized they needed assistance. A split second later I came to the conclusion we would be unable to help.

Out of the corner of my eye, I saw Alex turning to help; he flipped and his kayak drifted with him to the opposite shore where he ended up safe in an eddy. We managed to find an eddy a short distance from where the kayak was trapped. As we came in, Richard was just coming into the same eddy when his kayak flipped. We never really understood the reason why his kayak flipped that way. He managed to stay with the kayak and reach shore where he pumped out the water. In the middle of the river, we saw Charlotte float by accompanied by assorted gear. We were in no position to help.

Seconds later, Alex re-entered his water-laden kayak to paddle around a point where the safety rafts were located. He flipped again, trapped against a tree. Sacha arrived in time on the safety raft and tossed out a tow rope. For the next few minutes it was a fight against the water. The kayak was extracted from the tree and floated to the area where the rafts were tethered. A raft was dragged through the woods on the opposite bank.

Much shouting followed and Tom was told to head in our direction. Sometime later, he stumbled through the thickets of alders. He appeared to be in shock for he had been in the water for who knows how long. It should be pointed out the river is fed by glaciers and is very cold. He asked, "Where's Charlotte?"

Our response, "We don't know."

The raft came over and the crew went to salvage the kayak still hanging in the tree. Tom, in the meantime, stopped shivering. Alarm bells went off in our heads. We realized he was now hypothermic. He started removing his PFD and spray skirt. We shouted, "Keep them on for they will keep you just a bit warmer." He did up his PFD. I think it dawned on him he was in no position to make any rational judgments.

The crew retrieved the kayak. Its broken struts were bent out of shape and the chines (the spine) had snapped. It was piled on the raft. We were to kayak over to where the remainder of the group had gathered. Olaf told us, "We are going to a fishing camp some 500 metres downstream so that those who need to can dry out. The hypothermic cases are to be treated."

By the time we arrived, Tom was in a cabin and in a sleeping bag with a stove going full tilt. We were dry and in no immediate danger, so took our time unloading and moving into a cabin. Tom had severe hypothermia which is considered to be extremely dangerous. It took about 15 hours before he warmed up.

Later, we learned from Tom that he thought he was a goner. He couldn't figure out which way was up. He gulped water and in doing so saw a branch above him. He reached up and managed to get some air. But he remained in the water for an unknown time. Charlotte had managed to free herself, but in doing so lost a paddling boot and because of having a sock under a gasket her pants filled with water.

Lessons learned:

Keep your head when kayaking down a raging river; wear protective gear and use it correctly. We were fortunate we stayed upright, were wearing our paddling gear and we had stayed dry.

D. SANDY NIELSEN - I

Exciting Tales of the Far-West World with Thorval:
First of the Steel-Blades and his Blood Brother
Mingeegook: Last of the Mo-Mic-Thuks
Rousingly Bold Adventurous Sagas;
With awe, myth and magic too!

Rousing Foreword

Of course, Thorval made it to the New World. Wasn't he the main character and motivator in the Vinland Sagas?

No, I guess not. That part must have been omitted by an astute ancient editor. Not a problem, I've gone and included it here.

The Vikings went everywhere and saw everything on the endless oceans. They travelled to the endless sands of the Sahara, the endless rivers of the Volga and others, as well as the endless glaciers of Greenland. They were at the great cities of Baghdad, Constantinople and Rome, the Eternal City itself. They had contact with the hordes from the East.

Was there anything left to see?

The New World was just that, a whole new world; endless. The Vinland Saga probably only covered a portion of their travels. They didn't have a reporter or news correspondent on board all ships. They probably didn't even 'tweet' each other. It could be the fanciful speculations told about their journeys just aren't fanciful enough. If you go to a supermarket and you don't find apples, that doesn't mean that apples never ever existed. (Perhaps pickled herring would be a better analogy.)

Anyhow, I've never tried to make Thorval anything less than fanciful.

Adventurous Saga No. 1

Pressure

As ants they were, from the distance; so numerous; perhaps lemmings. Thorval had never seen their like. The Skræling Chief, who laid beside him in the brush of the rocky mount, smiling, had been right. He had never seen anything like this.

This was a voyage past Liefer's settlement, down the massive river, and through the vast freshwater seas, past the Eetchieglümie, and into this endless land of Skrælings, via portages and rivers. This sight, in itself, was worth it and he knew that he was still in Midgård, the world of men. This, though, was something he would have only thought to have seen in one of the other Nine Worlds, like Alfheim, or Vanaheim.

"Thorval glad happy be? I right, no? Good to see? We move down closer. See better," Mingeegook spoke his gallimaufry of clipped Norse that he had picked up, quite well, "Never see so many; huh?"

"I've seen torsk, cod, like that off Lief's landing, but they were fish."

"Blood brother, see animal like this before?" Mingeegook asked as they moved closer and a stray came close. They were many, he was the last, no Mo-Mic-Thuks.

Thorval had to shout over the sound like thunder, "They are like Trolls' cattle." The Skræling Chief laughed and leaned in to Thorval's ear saying, "No like cow."

Thorval coughed from the cloud of dust the thundering hoofs had kicked up, "Perhaps there was something like it out by the Tartar lands, their buffalo."

Thorval looked out over the vast sea of grass that stretched out forever just like the land of the Huns and Tartars. The cloud of dust that the herd had kicked up rose high into the sky. When he got back home, or even Lief's Landing, no one would believe his tales of these huge innumerable beasts thundering across a plain as far as the eye could see. Thousands upon thousands that Mingeegook had told him could take three days to pass. How the Skrælings of this land would run some off the cliff for food, and make everything from the beast they needed. These huge, haired and hunchbacked . . . ogre-cattle were fearsome indeed with their curved horns. Thorval wondered if he could get a few horns to mount on helmets to scare any foemen.

Still in all his travels on the turbulent seas of Midgård, or all the Nine Worlds, he doubted that he would ever see a sight such as this; one that was so, so full of – life. Yah, this herd had so much life, so much power and force, the gods themselves would never be able to stop them, they as a whole, were an entity in themselves. This spectacle would be burned in his mind forever; first and foremost from now on.

Mingeegook hit him in the arm – hard. Thorval looked at him and saw something like extreme tenesmus on his features. Ney, it was something he had never seen in the fierce warrior's face before – fear. Worse than that; it was an unabashed terror, a dread. He grabbed Thorval by the arm and dragged him down the crag to where there was a cleft in the rock of the hill. It led to a cave and Mingeegook pushed Thorval inside. Deep inside, they turned around and looked out over the endless herd of great brutes.

Thorval couldn't see what had scared the unafraid Chief, though he did seem far more relaxed now within the rock. Everything was the same outside. The herd rumbled by as before, the dust of their passage rose to the air, but still there was something altered about their demeanour. They too seemed to have a panic about their hurtle across the plain, now it was more like a stampede, though everything seemed the same. Thorval shrugged to indicate he was still at a loss to what had set such fright into Mingeegook's soul.

Mingeegook pointed out over the herd, but Thorval couldn't see a thing. Mingeegook jerked his arm upwards and Thorval looked up above the cloud of dust and saw something that was sucking the grime up into the sky. Something huge. Something totally fearsome. It was like the whirling dervishes that would dance their jigs across the water at times, or the hot sands of the lands south. Yet this was worse than any wind he had seen on land or sea. It dwarfed any waterspout he'd beheld. It was like the formidable maelstrom off the North Way's coast, but of air, not sucking its victims down, but up.

A thousand times faster and a thousand times larger. And a thousand, thousand times more horrific. Thorval wondered if his own god Thor and his mighty hammer Mjolinir, and goats, Toothgnasher and Toothgrinder, could whip up a storm of such fierceness and magnitude, nor if they could defeat it.

"What is this?" Thorval shouted over the amplified roar of hooves and storm.

"Great evil spirit of land, maybe Wind-he-go. Great spirit."

"I believe that. I've seen Surt spew forth his fire and ash in Iceland, but nothing like this."

Thorval's jaw dropped, before he quickly closed it to stop the flying filth that entered the cave from getting into his mouth. He watched awestruck as the herd he had considered as an unstoppable force of nature in itself was lifted up off the floor of the grasslands and twirled violently upwards into the swirling vortex, the bawling of the creatures drowned out by the destructive whirlpool of vicious wind currents. The base of the funnel moved haphazardly across the land, but with the land covered in the shaggy brutes, everywhere it moved they were swept up in its immutable hurling grip. A spirit of the sky and air that showed no mercy, no leniency. Clemency was not for the dark spirits that abided here.

Could it be a brace of Valkyries, a rage of huntresses, a boast of reapers, on the hunt gathering meat for the feast of the Valhal from their larder – ney.

And as quickly as it seemed to have started the funnel rose back into its malevolent home in the sky and a clear peaceful blue reigned the heavens once again. Thorval thought that he had now seen the sight of sights, then the dark clouds disgorged their contents and it rained great shaggy beasts.

Mingeegook headed out between the rock walls, but Thorval was apprehensive, and well shaken, if only in the mental sense. The howling winds on the seas whipping up mountainous swells had never bothered him, not like this. This was something different. Still, Mingeegook was assured and encouraged him out.

They headed out to survey the damage. Thorval's hand held tight to the hilt of his sword, though futile against such forces, it gave him comfort. The path of destruction was evident where the malicious spirit had passed, grass and scrub ripped out from the roots. The indestructible creatures lay broken and battered, lifeless across the landscape. Soon they would be food for carrion-eaters, vultures, flies, and fertilizer for the torn vista.

Thorval had always known that the forces of nature, the environment, were more fearsome than any mere god. He had seen it on the waves of the northern seas. He had seen it on the ice sheets of the Greenland. He had seen it on the ocean of sand, south of the Mid-Earth Sea. He had seen it on the quaking islands on the Mid-Earth Sea. He had seen it on the volcanoes and geysers of the Iceland. Now he had relearned this lesson again, though this time it was a tight wound wicked wind on land, which cleansed itself of the mortal insects in it path

Thorval wondered again if any of his fellow Norse would ever believe his tales. He doubted it. These vast tracts of sward ripped free of the earth, now littered with the heavy creatures that had just thudded back to the ground.

Mingeegook had cut free a couple of the thick tongues from their gaping mouths with his flint blade and had already somehow managed to start a quick fire to cook them.

"Can we get back on the waters again?" He looked to his companion as they examined the trail of devastation.

"Soon," Mingeegook stated in his stoic manner. "Soon."

Addendum:
Approximately: 60 million bison, circa 1000 A.D.

Adventurous Saga No. 2

Light Might

When the Skræling hurled the spear with all his might, Thorval side-stepped it, grabbed the shaft, spun, and flung it back at his aggressor. His assailant did not return it to Thorval, deciding to keep it, lodged deep in his heart as it was. He fell forward lifeless; the shaft of the spear hit the hard earth causing the tip to come out his back as his cadaver slid forward.

Mingeegook leapt to his feet while raising his flint axe, knowing what was going down, other than the fallen warrior, but another of the fallen one's tribe had also risen and tapped him on the back of the head with a gnarled cudgel, knocking him blank out.

Thorval reached for the hilt of his steel-blade, but the natives of this Kanata, this lodge, rose up around them from their seated position and held him fast. They had not believed his rantings, nor cared, now that he had killed their main warrior. Still he blustered, "Look at the white colour of my skin. I am a god; the son of Thor, named after him. See my blond hair, I am a great spirit. My beard is red from eating flesh the likes of Skrælings."

Words though they were, they were nothing more than grunts and groans to the natives of this Kanata, these Kanatask, without Mingeegook to translate. Perhaps it was the way his companion had translated. Perhaps not. It had done no good. Skrælings were bird-brained, evident from the feathers in their head-bands.

The native so apt with his cudgel tapped him on the back of his head. Thorval's false claims ceased as his fair head nodded forward.

Awakening, hands strapped securely behind to a thick upright stake, Thorval shook his golden mane in the dark night. He could see by the campfire, that Mingeegook, staked like himself, was awake. They both had brush heaped about their feet, to be burned alive.

Thorval's fingers couldn't reach the hilt of his sword, the natives not knowing what it was in its sheath, had secured it along with him. Thinking of nothing else, Thorval blustered again, with Mingeegook explaining.

"Your spirits are nothing compared to my god, Thor. He is the god of storms; the god of thunder and lightning." He struggled with his bonds as did Mingeegook. His hammer is mighty and his chariot drawn by fierce goats cause the sky to thunder."

Mingeegook had an expression of heap big tenesmus, the wide open sky being clear and filled with dim stars. There were no storms on the horizon. The leaves of nearby trees, still, from lack of even a breeze.

The natives were restless. They paid no attention to Thorval's rants or more specifically Mingeegook spewing forth his translations in a loud torrent, near a storm in itself.

"Fowl Skrælings. You know not what wrath you have wrought against the Norse gods. Thor the god of thunder will smite you down with one of his lightning bolts if you do not release us now.

The Kanatask Skrælings paid no heed, preparing now to revel in burning their captives alive. The red glowing firelight intensified the flame in their eyes.

Mingeegook had worked a hand free and was groping for a piece of sharp flint in a pouch, trying to remain unseen, but it was too late. "Free us now and live," Thorval threatened ineffectually, as a Skræling approached with a brand to set alight their funeral pyre, alive or not.

Then it happened. Thor responded.

Night was day as a silent lightning bolt filled the clear moonless night. It did not flash away as it had come into existence. It stayed as a broad luminescent sail fluttering in the heavens, illuminating all. The wretched ones fell to their knees in fear of the Norse god lest he should smite them all down.

Mingeegook reached the keen flint and cut his bonds then his companion's. Thorval freed, and irked, unsheathed his steel-blade in a flow of motion, up and down, effectively separating the bowed head of the Kanatask chief from his shoulders.

The other Skrælings inched away on their haunches like cowered dogs.

"Halt!" Thorval kicked the head away with his boot. "Now do you believe?" He pointed with his silvered cutting edge to the radiance in the firmament. "Will you obey me and Mingeegook?"

They ceded in abject dread of the blinding sorcery well beyond their ken.

"Your best food and drink. Your best blankets and furs for us to sit upon. After that your finest daughters, washed clean, for us to enjoy ourselves upon. Obey me now." Thorval commanded via Mingeegook's shouts, his steel-blade held high.

The wretched ones, in a fear previously unbeknownst to them scurried to heed tasks at hand. They knew not whether to fear the shimmering sheet of stationary lighting, unlike any of their Northern Lights, or the strange cutting blade that sparkled above their heads, having effectively decapitating their, once was, head man, in one leisurely swoop.

The women set up soft furs for them to sit upon and gave their finest food to eat.

Mingeegook leaned towards Thorval, saying in his gallimaufry of Norse, "You tell me you believe not in any god many time. Many time you tell me if there gods, they care not about man, or you." He took a bite of venison and chewed it and swallowed before continuing. "But Thorval blood-brother, I tell you something truth. Your god sure believe in you and sure care about you. How you get him do this?"

"I didn't. I still don't believe. I was as scared as them but I knew enough to take advantage of the situation."

"You call that Lief, Luck-man, no so much some be you Thorval." Mingeegook asked, "What be wait lightning bolt? Still stuck in sky."

Thorval shrugged and raised his arms to the sky, "A freak Northern Light? I don't know."

He spat out some food he didn't like. "Think we're safe to sleep?" The short squat bolt was poised; ready.

"Plenty safe. They too scared."

The Kanatask brought the girls for them to choose from.

"Tell them to take the children away and bring women. And Thor's light sees all." Thorval reclined, closed his eyes. He could sleep without a night light, or with, drained as he was.

He pondered things such as Æsir and Norns. Even the gods feared the Three Sisters of Fate; if any of them existed. His own life was often of the wyrd.

Addendum:
The explosion of the Crab Nebula super nova illuminated the night sky on July 4th 1054 A.D. and was visible during daylight for three days.

Adventurous Saga No. 3
Clouded

"Memories," Thorval said, "Yah, for certain. Gather round me and my companion," he pointed to Mingeegook. "Come out of the smoke yet close to the fire to stave off the cold of this star filled night, a night for stories as such, before you head to your beds. You also young women, come close. My crew will not hear of this again as they have heard it too often, and believe it not."

The children and women too, gathered about in the lee of the sod longhouse in the new frontier of Vinland. Pulling woollen cloaks about them on a warm night with a cool breeze off an arctic current, they settled on long smooth logs of driftwood hauled from the beach. Their ears doted on any syllable that issued from Thorval's lips, while their eyes kept vigil on Mingeegook.

"Remember all as I told you that last eve of how my Skræling comrade and I had travelled into to the heart of this great land, and the thousands upon thousands of bison that swept across the vast grasslands only to be sucked up by a great swirling Wind-ee-go." The enthralled barely nodded under their fleece covers; Thorval standing, his arms in a twirling motion.

"I was appallingly troubled by this mystic land, but Mingeegook convinced me to carry on. Ever stalwart." Thorval pointed to Mingeegook, his eyes agleam in deep multiple bags, as he swilled deep of Norse Vinland wine.

"Further west into untouched prairies we went. The swards, as high as our heads, except for where the great shaggy horned creatures had thundered across the plains, to graze." Thorval, occasionally paused to let his audience recall his previous tale's descriptions and ponder the new. "Oh, how I wished for a sturdy Icelandic pony to save wear on my feet.

"A tribe of friendly Skrælings welcomed us, engrossed by my pallid pallor as always. Mingeegook told them I was some form of god, or such." Thorval shrugged in the flickering light.

"These Skrælings would misdirect some of the shagged beasts off a cliff, to dash them to their deaths, and use every piece of the brutes. We indulged ourselves with the natives in a beast feast. The time was good. There was much celebration." A pause. A look to the listeners in each of their flame flickering pupils. "And fights." The crowd waited with bated breaths, the fish they had consumed for dinner made it smell like baited breaths.

"They dared not fight me, deity they believed me to be." His hands rose to the vault of glittering stars. "But many did fight Mingeegook that sunny mid-day." He swung on one foot with flourish. "No weapons, it was all in good fun. Mingeegook, need I say, beat all comers. A true champion." Thorval indicated his hero companion on that far journey.

Mingeegook raised an arm in victory, then fell off the stump onto the earth – sound asleep – dead drunk - on Norse wine made from the native grapes.

"He deserves his rest." No one moved to move him. He looked like a leather sack full of cod thrown on the dock.

Thorval wove on. "The Skrælings laughed hard and hearty, their bellies full. Then one looked to Mingeegook, his face filled with dread. Mingeegook was puzzled. I could see nothing fearsome about the warrior - nothing new. But it was not Mingeegook. His opponent was looking over his shoulder to the west." A halt in the tale, then, "Do you know what he saw on the horizon?"

"The evil spirit! The twisting demon! The Wind-ee-gook!" were the responses shouted out by the children – women too, caught up as they were in the tale, and some trying to catch the adventurer's eye.

"So believed I, yah-yah, for the sky was covered. Though it seemed not to swirl as before, but perhaps it was gathering strength.

"The Skrælings forgot I was one to be deified, and grabbed myself and Mingeegook, before we had time to protest and many hands dragged us down the cliff and shoved us into a large cave, where a great, smoky fire was hurriedly built at the mouth." There was silence except for the occasional crackle of an ember.

"And a sound, a sound like none ever heard before."

Mingeegook snorted loud in his sleep and several jumped.

"Ney, not that sound. Have you ever heard the sound of a tight rope in a strong wind of a drakkar humming?"

All had.

"It was something like that, but a thousand times louder. It filled the ears with sound until there was no more room and it pushed into ones' very skulls, and we held them with our hands." Thorval demonstrated, the children followed suite, unconsciously.

Taking down his hands he continued, "Yet it was not a spinning wind that descended upon us. There was no wind at all. That which covered the horizon, that which deafened us, that which descended on all – was – a swarm. It was a swarm of insects. A plague of locusts had descended upon the land, such as the priests in the Church of the White Christ bespake of happening in those far off days.

"They ate everything beyond our wall of smoke." Thorval looked to each and all with a saga-teller's intensity. "There were as many as there were sand grains on the White Strands south of here.

"Through the fuliginous barrier and under the deafening cicada buzz we could hear the vast eternal herd of shaggy bison bemoaning the fact their dominance of the land had been displaced by mere bugs. We could hear them thundering overhead in our cavern; on the move once more. I imagined them on the hoof as their bushy coats and flesh was stripped from them being devoured to the bones." Pause. "Shiny ivory white skeletons, thundering across the plains, endless, as yet unaware they were dead." Thorval knew the mothers would be irked with him once more as their born would be unable to sleep another night; this image seeded. Yet perhaps one of the young women would need comfort this eve.

"The Skrælings huddled at the back of the cavern, jabbering amongst themselves, in worrisome terror, that much was obvious, yet Mingeegook," a snort from the sleeping Native as if he had heard his name, "could make no sense of their language and signs." Thorval fluttered his fingers around and about in the firelight to express the locusts.

"Three days the Skrælings kept us in that hole in the cliff, relating tales of their elders; elders' memoirs of such things. The buzzing diminished. The locust with nothing more to eat moved on. We went back into the world once more and to the top of the cliff. It was a barren landscape. The grass that was above our heads - was no more. Not even stubble remained. The bare soil was littered with dead insects. The locust had only devoured the vegetation, but now there was nothing for the bison to eat, so most moved on looking for more verdant fields, as yet untouched.

"We had more, ney, too much to eat, as many of the shaggy beasts had stampeded blind over the cliff; a mad dash to death. They were heaped in a massive squirming pile, many not yet dead. The Skrælings began work on hides, not wanting to waste, before rot set in.

"I had heard from the White Christ priests of the plague of locusts long ago, but had passed it off as so much propaganda; as most of their religion is. We bided our time with this tribe and helped dry meat and cure hides in this desolate landscape, knowing naught what to expect if we moved further west. Indeed the interior of this great land was daunting to the most unfaltering. Give me the cold northern seas, them I know.

"In all the Nine Worlds there was naught to surprise me, ice of the Greenland, fire of the Iceland, monster waves stirred of the deep; I had seen it all. Then it happened." Thorval slammed the axe of suspense into the air above and let it hang there, embedded in their imaginations. He dropped his hands to his sides and stood still as a crag. Memory. He let them wait to build suspense. Wait they did. A series of loud snorts from Mingeegook, finally broke the silence, and Thorval continued.

"I had thought the first outbreak of locust was beyond belief. The next one that came from the west made the first not worth mentioning. The horizon was dark all the way south to all the way north. It went from the soil of Midgård, high to the very roots of Asgård itself. It blocked half of everything. And there was nothing left to eat this time, except the very meat on our bones.

"Again the Skrælings hustled us down into the cave and blocked the entrance with as much leafless brush as they could, pushing it together tight, till very little light penetrated. This time though they did not set fire to it to keep the locust at bay.

"We waited." Thorval too paused, his listeners distracted by Mingeegook's quite loud snorts – or perhaps this time farts – as he lay like a bag of semi-live halibut.

"The buzz was higher pitched this time and very grating. Perhaps it was not locust, but a different insect set forth by a munificent god in this land, to devour the first.

"The mouth of the cave darkened further and dust and sand blew in making us all cough. It was not insects at all this time." Pause – look. "It was sand. It was a sand storm the likes of which never had been seen before by any living Skræling, but told of in legends handed down from the distant past.

"It was if the sand from all the beaches in the all the Nine Worlds were set aloft and powered by the fiercest of gales. After its passing we headed forth again. It scoured and scrubbed an already besieged landscape clean, making the old lava flows of Iceland seem as a Vanir paradise. The bison that had remained in the area were now dead, the exterior of their hides, blasted clean of fur. Mingeegook took his knife and cut open the lungs of one." The fire continued to crackle. "Dried sand issued forth from it."

Another gasp flowed from the bunch, followed by some involuntary coughing.

"Having talked to our own ancient wise men afore, my thoughts are such. It is known that at times Ymir the King of Ice Giants blows his mighty breath down from his throne in the far north, and Surtur, in the unknown south retaliates by blowing his breath up. When they meet, a wind is set rolling across the land as if to blow away mountains.

"I believe that a wind as such came across the lands that the locust had previously decimated and picked up all the bare dirt from there setting it to motion in a gargantuan spindrift, that reached as high as the eye of the sun, leaving it red for many a day.

"I do not think I can recommend the settling of this land by our peoples as I had previously promoted. Perhaps it is best we hoist our sails and head home; truly.

"The bison appeared to be innumerable and unassailable. The spinning, sucking, storm was unthinkable. The locust swarms were unimaginable. And the sand storm was totally inconceivable." In sotto voce, "How can I recommend we settle this land?"

Thorval stopped, clapped his hands together and said, "That's all. Good night. Sleep well and easy." He sniggered to himself, knowing they would be up for many a long hour.

The young woman whom Thorval had been keeping a bit more of an eye on stood, and faced him. He smiled warmly at her as she said, "Lots of storms." Her voice oozed cynicism, "Sand is not what you are full of Thorval."

She stormed off too – out of memory – almost.

BALA MENON - I

Is That You, Ethel?

"Ethel," he shouted. Or was it 'Hazel'?

Old Johnny was grumpy today. The vehicle crossed the Queensway-Dundas intersection and turned right, picking up speed.

"Is that my wife over there? Tell her to get over here. Whom is she talking to?" he shouted again. There was only the hum of the engine and a distant sound of road traffic.

"Ah, we are on the Agawa Canyon Train," Johnny mumbled. "This is a fun ride. We were on this train more than 60 years ago. We cuddled and kissed and I became as hard as the granite of the King Mountain in the Algoma Highlands. Do you remember that, Ethel, eh? Awesome, awesome!"

Potholes on the road made the ride a bit bumpy. "Heh, heh, heh," Old Johnny laughed, as he bounced up and down.

"And in the Agawa River, do you remember, Ethel? We waddled in and saw otters making love, twisting and turning and you wanted to do the same?" His words were incoherent.

"And we sure did. Yes, we sure did, on the bank of the stream," Old Johnny was ecstatic. "We saw two children watching us from behind a bush and we shouted at them, 'Shoo, shoo, go away'. Like this, like this." Johnny wiggled his fingers.

"We walked along the Chapleau Trail, and oh my god, it had so many ancient trees. Maple and oak and aspen. The beams of sunlight were poking through the foliage. It was all gold and green and cool shadows. Have you forgotten?" His voice trailed away with a deep sigh.

"Your eyes are beautiful, Ethel. Remember, how I kissed them?" Old Johnny puckered his lips, blowing wet kisses into the air. "Squirrels? Oh yes, there were hundreds of them around. And chipmunks. You laughed when I chased those squirrels, running after them like this." Old Johnny was now flailing his legs about. Running, running.

The vehicle turned onto Highway 427 and accelerated as it sped northward. A horn sounded along with a brief burst of a siren.

"Where are you, Ethel? I can hear you talking. Whom are you talking to? Who is that man over there with you?" There were curtains across the windows and he craned his neck. He couldn't see anything and his neck ached.

Old Johnny was angry now. His hands had become fists and he was shivering. "Get over here, Ethel, get over here. I want you here." He tried to regain his breath. Wheezing, wheezing.

The paramedics in the ambulance were indifferent. They knew about Old Johnny. "I am returning him to his long-term care group home in Etobicoke," the driver told his partner. "Johnny has been in hospital with bronchitis for three weeks now."

The vehicle slowed, took a sharp turn to the right at the 427 and Burnhamthorpe intersection and crept eastward through the heavy evening traffic.

Old Johnny muttered something about being in a nickel mine elevator in Sudbury. "Slow, slow, Ethel...slow slow," his tone was relaxed as the words floated away.

"Some of the hospital staff think he is uttering gibberish the whole day, but if you listen closely you will know that he is telling a story," the driver said. "Now, listen carefully, he is mumbling 'Osha, Osha'. What he is saying is 'Awesome, Awesome'."

"What about his wife?" his partner asked.

"Yes, Janet, that was his wife's name. She is dead. Gone about six years ago, I think. Johnny doesn't remember much, you know. He is about 86 and we keep taking him to the Trillium Hospital every three months or so. He has this lung problem to compound his other ailments."

"Johnny is quite a star at the group home. If he hears a woman's voice, he thinks it is somebody called Ethel. On some days, it could be Maria, on other days it is Sandra or June or Alice and he calls out to them. He gets all vigourous and then has to be strapped onto his bed."

"He must have been a real wolf in his days," the paramedic said, drawing the window curtain aside and looking at Old Johnny.

The Global Positioning System (GPS) mounted on the dashboard droned again, the recorded female voice saying, "Take a turn to the left, 10 metres, then turn right after 20 metres. Your destination is on the left."

Lying on his stretcher at the back of the vehicle, his arms secured by leather straps, Old Johnny squirmed and giggled.

BALA MENON - II

Stranger On The Lawn

I clearly remember that warm and sunny afternoon on a spring day last year. It was Thursday, April 11, at around 3:30 pm.

I had taken the day off from work and was on the front lawn of my large home in one of the new sub-divisions in Castlemore, on the north-east side of Brampton.

I was digging holes to plant some of those fancy *hostas* or plantain lilies as they are called. These have attractive foliage and I knew they would look good around my five-year-old red maple tree. I also had a white hibiscus sapling, which I hoped would become a focal point in the arrangement.

The second hole had just been dug, when suddenly a dark shadow seemed to eclipse the sun. I looked up to see a man looming over me. I hadn't seen or heard him approach and I must admit I felt a terrible fear deep within me. I consider myself a man of deliberate thought and action and I don't like surprises.

The man had a black overcoat and a black fedora-like hat and must have been more than six-and-a-half feet tall. He was rather lean, although the shadow suggested a man of wider girth.

"Why on earth is he wearing an overcoat?" I thought. "It is so hot. And how did he get in? This is a gated, estate community."

I struggled to get up, but he placed his right hand on my left shoulder. It felt as though it weighed 30 or 40 lbs and I was forced to squat flat on the ground.

"Don't be afraid," he said. His voice sounded like a breeze rustling the reeds near a river bank and coming from somewhere far away. "I just want to speak with you. Something very important to me and my family."

There was a hint of menace in his voice. I couldn't see his full face, because the sun was behind him and his hat was low on his forehead. He stretched out his arm. "My God," I muttered. His arm seemed almost 10 feet long as he pointed to my house and said: "This is my home."

I pushed his hand away and got up. He seemed to get taller, his shadow still looming over me. "This is my home and has been with my family for more than 200 years," he whispered.

This guy is mad, I thought. I bought this house five years ago directly from the builder and have been punctual with my mortgage payments. Nonsense.

"This guy is mad. I bought this house five years ago directly from the builder and have been punctual with my mortgage payments. Nonsense." I realized with a thump in my heart that he was able to convert my thoughts into speech and I was involuntarily talking out aloud.

"Scoundrel," I thought again. And he made me say it aloud, "Scoundrel."

"Holy cow," I thought. And loud again, "holy cow."

"I don't like the tone of your thoughts, sir," his voice was now huskier, as if the reeds were swaying in the wind. The warmth of the late afternoon vanished.

"I can be an ugly man if you want me to be one." He shook what looked like a foot-long finger near my nose.

"You cannot plant this sort of garbage on my land." He stomped on the *hosta* I had just planted. "You have to plant corn now and spinach in the off-season. And I see that you have erected this monstrosity over the foundation of my home. Where are the lovely chimneys and the small tower with its little windows that was over the attic? Where is the red tiled roof and where is the ivy?"

"I climbed the tower every evening to see the sunlight spread a golden blanket over the farm," his voice was fainter. The breeze was dying in the reeds. "This is where my family lived for three generations and I will take steps to repossess my home." He paused, leaned closer to me and whispered, "I can be a bad man." A smell, akin to the one that I have breathed in occasionally along the Humber river, blasted my nostrils. A damp and earthy smell.

I was experiencing a panic attack now. I bent down and picked up the shovel, ready to defend myself.

The shadow disappeared. The man in the overcoat and hat was moving towards my house. He looked like a runaway horse, taking five to six strides at a time. "Hey!" I shouted. "Stop!" I gave chase, but was far behind when he pushed the door open and disappeared into the house.

I approached with caution, fearing he could be hiding behind the door or the powder room, ready to pounce on me. I held the shovel aloft and shouted "Hey, get out of my house. Come on out, come on out."

It was good there was nobody home. My children were at school and my wife was at work. I crept into the living room. Where did he go? I looked behind the sofas and then went into the kitchen, where I picked up a butcher's knife as well. One never knows how these kind of events end. It's better to be safe. I shuffled through the dining room and the family room. There was no sign of the man.

I took the stairs, a step at a time. He has to be upstairs in one of the five bedrooms. "My God, should I call 911?" I said to myself. "Or, am I imagining things? Was there really a man? Let me find him, anyway."

I went through all the bedrooms, washrooms, looking under

the beds, in the closets and behind the curtains. He couldn't enter the attic; it was padlocked from below.

I even looked into shoeboxes and dresser drawers. "Maybe he shrank himself to hide. It is a strange world we live in." I found all the windows locked, so he couldn't have jumped outside. Where did he go?

I must tell you about the odour of pipe tobacco that I encountered when chasing the man into my house. It was very strong on the top floor and on the stairs. I heard a slight sound, a pitter-patter of feet, as if a child or a small dog was running across a hardwood floor. I rushed down the stairs, through the family room, the kitchen, the dining room, the living room and into the foyer where I stopped dead. My skin crawled.

The evening light was streaming through the frosted glass panels on my front door. It was golden-hued and I could see the dust specks floating towards me. Imprinted on one of the glass panels was a silhouetted figure of a man in profile, wearing a wide-brimmed hat, with his coat collar turned up and a pipe in his mouth. It was the same man!

The story fascinated many of my friends who came by. They shook their heads and agreed that there are many things in this world and under the stars that we don't know about. "Let the glass panel stay as it is; maybe it has magical powers; maybe it will protect your home," they opined. "Why tinker with the unknown?" The door and its glass panel, thus, became a talking point in our circle.

Three weeks went by before the secret got out.

I was coming down the stairs one evening and overheard my son telling one of his friends: "My dad bought this stained glass panel at the Brampton Flea Market, you know, the one on Airport Road and Steeles. A real bargain, he paid just 30 dollars for it. Look at the exquisite detail on the hat and the pipe and just look at the man's Adam's apple!"

BALA MENON - III

The Head Game

"Can you help me unscrew my head?" the passenger beside me on the Bluehorse bus said, elbowing me with some force.

We had got onto the bus at the company's terminal in Toronto and were off to New York. The bus was only about half full. Maybe it was the heavy snowfall of the previous night that deterred travellers. I was listening to a song on my I-pod and the man had been scribbling in a small black book for the past 40 minutes or so.

We had just made the turn off at the Hamilton-Niagara fork on Highway 403 when he elbowed me. I tried to move closer to the window when he poked me again; this time he had an 8-inch screwdriver in his left hand. "Yes, you will help me..." It was more a statement than a request.

"What?" I said. "What do you want?" I was getting scared now, my heart stepping up its tempo. So this is what fear is, I thought.

The passenger was calm, as if he was just somebody sitting on a park bench on a sunny spring afternoon, watching children whizzing past on roller blades or young mothers with strollers or couples walking hand in hand.

Outside, the snow was whipping up a ruckus, falling thick and fast. The traffic was slowing down to a crawl. Should I shout out to the conductor and move to another seat?

"Don't panic," my neighbour whispered. "And don't get up or change your seat. I might get angry and my head will explode, you know. I could bust your gut."

I dared not look into his eyes. "Look sir, I don't understand what you are saying. I am a simple man, I am a family man, I have two small children. Please let me go to another seat."

"Hey, hey," his voice was soothing. The other passengers might have thought we were having a pleasant conversation. He was almost a foot taller than me and muscular. I crouched further into my seat.

"Hey, just listen. I need your help to unscrew my head. That is all I am asking you to do. That is why I have this screwdriver. There are copper screws that go deep into my cranium, through each of my ears."

"Do you understand?" he continued, his voice dropping. "Let me make it simpler. Three years ago, I realized that this head on my shoulders is not my head." He touched his forehead. "This head that I have carrying around for 34 years is not my head. Somebody made a terrible mistake. Heads were transposed. And I have been searching for my property, my head, for the past three years."

"I have travelled across the country, to the small fishing ports on the east coast and the inlets on the west coast. I have gone to lakeside resorts, to ski slopes, to the beaches, to mountain parks and have gone on buses, the railroad and on ocean cruises in search of my head."

My stomach was tight with fear as I stared at the monster screwdriver in his hand. A chill crept up my spine.

"Are you listening?" he said, elbowing me again. I winced. "Sorry," he said, "I don't want to hurt you. I know you will help me."

"A month ago," he continued, "I saw a man on the Sherbourne subway platform." He paused and took a deep breath. "And he had my head on his shoulders. Can you imagine my happiness? Can you? I was ecstatic. My three-year search had come to an end. I followed him onto the road, past the St. Luke's church and then onto Silkweed Lane and saw him enter one of the apartment buildings. I knew what I had to do."

"A week later, I was occupying one of the apartments on the same floor. His name was Andrew. Yes, Andrew and he had a nice family, a wife and two children, the eldest about five years or so. Yes, a nice Ontario family."

"And t_t_then...then?" I stuttered.

His reply was brusque. "I hacked the head off. Last evening, I got him into my apartment and took possession of my head. The body is in my freezer."

We were approaching the Canada border post on Rainbow Bridge. "That head, my head, is wrapped in plastic and in the blue gym bag under my seat... it's a little bloody," he said, as I shuddered and whimpered. "We will now walk calmly to the washrooms and then you will help me attach my real head to my neck. We can then have pleasant conversation all the way to New York. By the way, my name is Sandro."

The driver manoeuvered the bus to a halt in a parking bay for security and passport clearance. Some passengers were getting off and Sandro tugged at my arm, picked up the gym bag and herded me to the exit.

What followed must have been high-octane drama. I leapt, ran, stumbled, fell, got up again and ran screaming to one of the booths. Several Canadian border officers rushed out, their guns drawn, ordering me to drop to my knees and throw my hands above my head. I was pushed to the ground, my jaw and chest bruising on the concrete. I felt a strong jolt of electricity pass through me.

I was handcuffed and dragged away to one of the cabins. Scores of people applauded the officers. They must have thought I was some kind of terrorist.

The border officers didn't believe my story. How could they? Sandro turned out to be a Brad Northmore, a make-up man with a theatre company in New York. His blue gym bag had some costumes and masks.

The rubber screwdriver which he had was a prop and couldn't hurt a fly; and he swore that he had not spoken to me at all and was busy on the bus with his notebook and pencil. Toronto police said everybody was accounted for in the solitary apartment building on Silkweed Lane. There was no missing person named Andrew and no body had been found in any freezer.

I have been charged with creating mischief under $5000 as per Criminal Code Section 430(4) and told to report at a police division in Toronto "for fingerprinting and processing", according to my case note. There is also a psychiatric evaluation and possible confinement mentioned.

I can't sleep at night, however. As Sandro or Brad got up to leave the Niagara interrogation room, I could see his lips move: "I will get you," as he made a slashing gesture across his throat. I am also having a problem with an intermittent buzzing in my ears. It began a few days ago. I have to find somebody soon to pull out these copper screws.

CLIFF TRAVERS - I

Not My Day

I have severe arthritis in both knees and hadn't slept well.

I didn't want to get up, but my doctor had told me that if I didn't walk for at least half an hour every morning, I soon wouldn't be able to walk at all.

I fell out of bed, got dressed, and looked out the window. It was overcast and there was a light drizzle coming down. I had a bad feeling about today - a premonition of trouble.

I left the seniors' building, where I live, and started down the street. I hadn't gotten very far, when a young man grabbed my arm and pulled me into an alley.

"Give me your wallet," he said. I gave him my wallet.

"Where are your credit cards?" he yelled.

"I don't have any credit cards," I replied. "I was just recently released from bankruptcy and won't have any credit for seven years."

He looked in the wallet again. "You don't even have an O.H.I.P. card."

"No," I replied. "I lost it last month, but I've applied for a new one. I should get it soon."

"There's no money in this wallet," he screamed.

"Oh, I keep my money in my coat pocket," I said.

"Give it to me or I'll kill ya."

I reached in my coat pocket and handed him the twenty-six cents.

His eyes bulged in their sockets. "Is this all the money you got?"

"Well yes. My old age cheques don't come until next week."

"I can't wait till next week. I need the money now."

"I'm very sorry," I said.

He was close to tears. "Why do you carry around an empty wallet?" he wailed.

"Oh it's not empty," I replied. "There's a secret compartment inside the wallet."

I pulled back the leather flap and he tore the picture out of the wallet.

"What the..?"

"It's a picture of my grandchildren," I said proudly.

His frustration boiled over. "They're as sorry looking as you," he cried. He stuffed the picture back into the wallet, threw it at me, and stalked off.

It took me quite a while to find the wallet. I broke my glasses before Christmas and I have trouble seeing.

I came out of the alley and continued my walk down the street. It was then that I slipped on a patch of ice, went way up in the air and landed on my backside. I couldn't move, the pain was so bad. I wished I had one of those things you see on TV that you push or squeeze when you've fallen and can't get up.

The pain was beyond belief as I struggled to my feet. I lost my temper.

"F... this!" I said, just as two old ladies from my seniors' building came by.

"What did he say?" one old lady asked the other.

"He said F... this!" the other replied.

"He must be drunk," the first one said.

I smirked as I hobbled away. I sure could use a glass of Guinness right now, but have to wait for some money until next week.

As I turned the corner, I saw a man beating up a woman. He pushed her against the wall and slapped her once, twice, three times in the face. If there's one thing I can't abide, it's a man hitting a woman.

"Stop that!" I said. I grabbed him and pushed him away from her.

The woman stopped crying and looked at me.

"Mind your own business, you old creep," she snarled.

"But he was beating you..."

"He's my husband. He can do whatever he likes."

She stepped forward and kicked me in the groin.

"Jesus, Mary, and Joseph," I said as I fell to my knees. The pain was excruciating.

The man and woman linked hands, laughed, and walked away.

I rolled on the ground. The area around my groin had gone numb. I couldn't feel anything. My privates had deserted the battalion. I struggled to my feet and headed for the seniors' home. I had done enough walking for one morning.

CLIFF TRAVERS - II

The Anna Greengabler Saga

Part One

WON'T YOU BE MY NEIGHBOUR?

Beautiful Neighbours Naked and *In The Mood Magazine*,
Brampton Edition,
8870 McLaughlin Rd. South,
Brampton, Ontario.

Dear Mr. Rogers,

I just picked up a copy of this month's edition of your magazine.

Imagine my horror, when I turned to page 17, and saw my picture. I was shocked and disgusted. It's not as though I had nothing to compare it to. For many years, I was a leading model in the magazine *Sunbathing for Health*. Although it was published in black and white only, I was told I looked beautiful because of the artistic use of rocks, sand and water.

Your magazine has made me a source of humour and probably ruined all chances I had for future work. I was assured by your picture editor that he would airbrush any blemishes which appeared in the picture. Instead, through the use of some kind of trick photography, he highlighted the small red pimple I have on the right side of my nose.

People have been calling all day asking if I have some sort of gigantic growth on my face. I had to point out to four people that I was nude in the picture. They hadn't noticed. When I think of what I had to do, to appear in your heinous rag. First, that creepy woman with the big box of tweezers and brushes. Then, that vulgar Hungarian gypsy who smoked those funny cigars as she cut, shaped and painted my toenails. And finally, that horrible, horrible man with the pounds and pounds of cocoa butter - his constant drooling.

And you, dear Fred, that was the sharpest cut of all. When you invited me to your place after the shoot, I thought you were a perfect gentleman. The distinguished way you took off your sport jacket, hung it carefully in the closet, and slipped on your cardigan.

I must admit I was a little uneasy when you introduced me to your world of make believe. I didn't feel comfortable riding on that little train around your house. But when you stopped in the kitchen and took out the dill pickles, the hard boiled eggs, the mayonaise, the Cool Whip, the king size bottle of strawberry jam, I knew it was time to leave.

I am giving serious thought to taking legal action!

Yours truly,
Anna Greengabler

The Anna Greengabler Saga
Part Two

ANNA TRIES AGAIN TO SHARE HER
BEAUTY WITH THE WORLD

SUNSHINE Girl
C/o *Toronto Sun* Photo Dept.
333 King St. E.
Toronto On. M5A 3X5

Dear Sir,

I do not know how this turmoil came to take place.

I sent my full length photo via e-mail to your photo department, as instructed, in my efforts to become a *Sunshine Girl*.

As I explained, the only appropriate picture I had was the black and white nude study, which a professional photographer had taken of me a few years ago. It is artistic and not at all pornographic. Rocks, sand and water are strategically arranged around my body so as to earn the clever title – Rocks, Sand and Body of Water. (Get it!)

Today, some individual, in a dirty mackintosh, appeared at my door, rang my bell, and attempted to gain entry. He kept saying he was from the police, but the badge he kept flashing at me looked like something one might retrieve from the bottom of a box of "Lucky Elephant Popcorn."

He kept asking me where on the beach the dead body was buried. He couldn't seem to comprehend that the picture was an artistic study of me and there was no dead body on my beach. He then asked if I was involved in 'snuff' films as he had heard such things were commonplace in my area.

I told him yes, there were several men of my acquaintance, who were snuff regulars, but most had given it up for health reasons.

When he heard this, he attempted to break the door down. I am afraid this proved to be his undoing as my next door neighbour came to my aid and asked what was going on. When this man said he was going to throw the crazy bitch (I suppose he meant me) in jail, dear Mr. Jenkins set his six pet alligators on him.

The alligators are quite harmless. They spend half of their time playing in the beach's sand and the rest of their time swimming in Mr. Jenkins's pool. They've all been registered with the city and all have legitimate dog licenses. Mr. Jenkins put his pets down as mongrels, but assured Animal Control there was no Pit Bull in their ancestry whatever.

In any case, this most disagreeable little man in the mac has not returned, so at least that's something.

If, however, I'm ever bothered again, about nude women supposed dead and buried in the beach somewhere, I will not hesitate to take legal action.

Yours truly,
Anna Greengabler

The Anna Greengabler Saga
Part Three

WHAT'S RIGHT IS RIGHT

Dollars for Gold,
257 Park Avenue South,
New York, N.Y., 10010.

Dear Sir,
Harold and I met in a little restaurant on the outskirts of Toronto many years ago. I was having scrambled eggs on toast. He was eating bangers and mash.

It was love at first bite! He wanted to marry me immediately. Unfortunately, he was already married, Catholic, and couldn't get a divorce.

So we did the next best thing. We went to Wasaga Beach for the weekend. It was pure rapture.

Harold worked for the government as a political negotiator. He carried a huge suitcase, filled with stocks, bonds and bundles of thousand dollar bills. The Monday, following our weekend, he had to fly to Finland to secure the release of a Swedish princess.

Before he left me, Harold took a ring off his left thumb. It was solid gold, with veins of platinum and was encrusted with large rubies, diamonds and sapphires. Harold told me to put the ring in a safety deposit box and keep it for a rainy day. Well, last month, it began to pour and hasn't stopped.

I had no other option. I sent you Harold's ring. I went out into the rain to mail it. This morning, I received your reply. There must be something wrong. Your cheque payable to me for goods received is for $1.75 U.S. Either your scales need repair or there is some kind of fierce typo. Perhaps, the cheque should have read $17,500 U.S.

Harold was an honourable man. My virtue was certainly worth more than $1.75 U.S.

I expect to hear from you soon. If not, I feel obliged to advise you that I am considering taking legal action!

Yours truly,
Anna Greengabler

CLIFF TRAVERS - III

Today Won't Come Again

TODAY

I rose early, showered, dressed, ate a healthy breakfast, checked my e-mails, strapped on my gun and left the house. She was now three days and three nights gone from my life. I resolved to put an end to the situation immediately. I knew where she was and whom she was with.

WON'T

I unlocked the door with the key that unlocks all doors. He refused to tell me where she was.

Denied all knowledge of her - carnal or otherwise. He said I had it all wrong.

COME

Her green eyes opened in disbelief. He had given her up in less than five minutes. All I had to do was show him the gun and he told me everything. She cried when I suggested she return home. Never, she said.

AGAIN

This place had been our home. Without her, it would be no one's home - ever again. I made her watch! She buried her face in her hands and whimpered softly as I burned the house to the ground.

Not This Time, Chester Morris

He sat beside her in the small fast food establishment. She didn't appreciate all the room he took nor his huffing and puffing. What irked her most was his bad breath and body odour.

She tried to get up, but couldn't because he was sitting on her skirt. She gently rapped his knee with her white cane.

He raised his left buttock and handed her a card. Macular degeneration had left her with less than ten per cent of her vision, but by pressing the card against her thick lenses, she was able to read: "I REQUIRE MONEY FOR FOOD. PLEASE HELP. ODD JOBS DONE."

"Please move or I'll call for help."

He handed her another larger card.

"DEAF AND DUMB," it read.

"Is this man bothering you?" a voice intruded.

"Yes, yes, he is."

"It's alright, friend. I was just leaving." Deaf and dumb, indeed!

She caught up with him a block down the street and slapped his face. He asked her if she couldn't take a joke and she replied he could go to jail for what he had done.

Still laughing, he took his mother by the arm and guided her up the stairs.

EVA BRUNEY - I

One Dumb Thief

It was 9:45 pm, that fateful Thursday night, when my doorbell rang. Putting aside the mop with a measure of annoyance and determination, I yanked open the front door.

I was going to give her a piece of my mind, my daughter that is, for missing her curfew.

Instead, a big burly brute was at the door. A big burly brute with a big ugly gun in his hand.

"Let me in and DO NOT SAY ONE WORD," the brute said.

I backed into the house, jaw down to the floor, eyes misting over, fear washing over every part of me.

My rubbery legs could hardly carry me back inside.

"Lock the door and turn off the lights," he said.

"What lights?" I asked.

"The porch lights, dummy."

I turned the lights off as demanded, all the while wondering, "What now? Now what?" Had I not been through enough?

"Who are you and what do you want?" hoping I appeared mighty brave. "Why are you doing this? I don't have much money, but you can have all of it and leave. Just take it. Go!"

The brute would have none of it. "Shut up and listen. I am not going anywhere. Not without you, that is. Where is your purse?"

"On the chair," I replied.

"Pick it up and show it to me."

"I told you I have no money," I said.

I walked or rather floated to where my purse lay on the chair, because by this time I really had no idea where I was. I felt like I was in another world. I attempted to hand the purse to the brute.

"Now open it," he said, "and hand me the ATM card."

"I...I..I don't have it."

"Where the hell is it then?" he asked.

"My daughter has it," I replied.

"What the hell for?" the damned brute wanted to know.

"My daughter is none of your business."

"I asked and I am not asking again. Where the hell is she?"

"I don't know, she did not say where she was heading."

"You people and your damned children. You let them do what they want and when they get in shit with the cops, you cry and wave your hands, hold your heads and complain about the law this and the law that, like you are the best parents in the world..."

"You shut up," I yelled, "just shut the damned hell up. You have no right to talk about the kind of parent I am. You know, I have had it with bastards like you. The other one ran off and left me with a ton of bills, and now you come demanding money? What a joke!"

"Who the hell else is here?" asked dumbass.

"I am alone, sheepface. All alone till my daughter returns."

No way was I letting him know that my seven-year-old son was sleeping upstairs.

"OK, I don't have all the time in the world. Get me all your jewellery," said sheepface.

"What damned jewellery? Have you looked around this place? The creaking floor, the kitchen door missing a hinge. Only one burner on the stove works... Take what you want and get the hell out. I have $79.00 in my purse for groceries. All is yours."

Now, I figured that if I played like a badass he would be fooled into believing I was one.

"You call me names and I am the one with the loaded gun. Right here in your house, in your face."

I threw the purse at his face. "Take it, take it all. At least, this time when I tell my banker I cannot meet the mortgage payment because I was robbed, it will be the truth."

"You know I am sick and tired of all you losers. All you jackasses do is take...take...take...why don't you get a job? I work at the pizza place around the corner...go get a job...dumbass..."

Ohhh, was I ever brave...I was just hoping that he did not pick up the tremble in my voice or see the puddle gathering at my feet.

"Woman, I have a gun, hear me, I have a gun...in your face..."

"Yes, I see your gun," and louder, "I SEE YOUR GUN, GUN GUN."

Then came the sweetest words I have ever heard... "DROP THE GUN AND LAY ON THE FLOOR!! DO IT NOW!! DROP THE GUN AND LAY ON THE FLOOR."

Whereupon the big, thieving brute dropped his gun and lay on the floor. With his arms outstretched. From this day on, I will not yell at Jason, my seven-year-old, when he is teaching his parrot words that he learned from the cop shows on television.

EVA BRUNEY - II

Never Too Late!

"Hello."

"Hi, girlfriend."

"Hey, Nancy, what are your plans for today?"

"I have not made plans, do you have something in mind?" I asked.

She went on to detail her day, which was very involved. Two malls and a movie.

Nancy is a mall person, I mean really. She lives in malls. Nancy can give directions to any store in any mall within a twenty mile radius of her home.

On the other hand, I hate shopping of any kind. If I need a dress from the mall, I will buy it from the first store I walk into that has my size. And that goes for slacks, jeans, shoes, everything. Since I did not have plans, I agreed to go with her.

"Okay, I will pick you up in half an hour."

"See you in thirty, Nancy."

I honestly see no purpose in walking the malls. I really do not.

Some people make a career of walking malls...I know this lady who goes to a big-box department store every morning and is picked up at six o'clock at night. I will never cease to wonder what she does there every day; she does not work there.

Well, Nancy picked me up and we were off to the mall. We drove around for about twenty minutes looking for a parking spot close to the entrance.

By this time, I was already tired and no longer interested in shopping; however, I had made a promise to Nancy. The first thing I do at any mall is head for the book store, so we decided that I would browse in the book store and meet in front of the card shop in one hour.

Nancy's parting words were, "Maybe you will meet your future today." She never said boyfriend or sweetheart; it was always 'your future'.

I began at the front of the store and worked my way to the back. Mind you, the books were so familiar to me I was simply strolling through. I picked up a book for my grandson and was paging through it on the way out. Time to meet Nancy again.

As I exited the store I crashed into a body, made my excuses and kept on going. I only know the body was male, had a hard chest and smelled divine. Why didn't I look at the face? I chided myself. What is the point anyway, they come...they go, such is my luck, so it makes no difference that I did not see the face belonging to the body. Man, did he smell delicious.

"Nancy, I just crashed into a man but I did not look at his face."

"You have to be kidding me, you didn't look at his face?"

"What is the point.. you know my luck with men."

"Maybe we will run into him again."

"Exactly, I will have to practically run into him to know him."

We stopped for coffee and as usual, I was being regaled with the great outfits and the unbelievable prices. Nancy, of course, had three bags and she was only halfway through her purchases.

"So, how tall is he? At least, you could judge that?"

"Well, I think my head came up to his chest."

"Why, for the life of me, would you not check him out?"

"Okay Nancy, let's finish up here and go see the movie."

"I just have to stop at the drug store for a minute."

We finished our coffee and headed for the drugstore. I waited outside and resumed turning the pages of the book I had picked up for my grandson.

Just behind me and to my right I heard this voice whisper, "Is it my turn to run into you?"

I whipped my head around and my eyes were level with a broad chest and he was standing so close, I knew it was that divine smelling bookstore man. My eyes travelled up to the face.

Talk about embarrassed, I did not know what to say, so I said, "Or run away with me."

Oh no, did I just say that? Please dig a hole and bury me! My face turned every colour imaginable, and man was I hot. I felt like I was in an oven.

He was calm and cool, as if he had not just rocked my world. We introduced ourselves and by that time Nancy had returned and introduced herself.

We chatted for a bit and then said our goodbyes, nice to meet you and so on.

All in all, the day was good.

Nancy drove me home and we promised to meet for lunch the next day.

We did meet for lunch at a small French cafe we both loved, and returned to work.

That evening my phone rang, and since I did not recognize the voice right away, I automatically assumed it was a telemarketer, said I was not interested and hung up the phone. I get so many of those calls, I do not bother to listen to their spiel anymore.

Had a nice long hot bath and curled up in bed to devour the latest novel I was so excited to see if I was right in my guess as to who the murderer was.

Into my sixth page now and I am so deep into the novel that I heard this noise and did not realize it was my phone. Oh boy, I was not happy.

"Hello."

"Hi, is this Angelique?"

"Who is asking?"

"I think we met at the mall, actually you ran into my chest at the bookstore, and we met at the drugstore. It's Gregory."

"Oh hi, how are you?"

"First, let me apologize for calling this late. You hung up on me before, so I did not get the chance to say who I was."

"Oh, that was you?"

I proceeded to apologise, and we had a short conversation.

Of course, I called Nancy as soon as we hung up, and found out she had slipped him my phone number.

"Well, are you going out with him?"

"Sure, we are going to a show and then dinner on Saturday."

Well, to cut a long story short, it has been twenty-seven years since that night. Twenty-six since we have been married. We have two sons and two daughters, and four grandchildren. Two boys and two girls and they never tire of hearing the story of how grandma and grandpa met, and as they say, long, long, long ago in ancient times.

EVA BRUNEY - III

I Go Places In My Mind

I go places in my mind
And always end up here with you
I think of where I want to be
Your arms are waiting there.

      I think of lips I want to kiss
      And yours are offered to me
      No matter where I am or what I do
      I always end up right back with you.

I think of songs I want to sing
Your face comes to my mind
I know the books I want to read
Your face is on every one.

      I think of arms wrapped around me
      And yours are open wide
      No matter where I go or what I do
      I always end up right back with you.

I'm longing for the moment when
I'm right back in your arms
To make up for the time I missed
When we were far apart.

      I'm hoping that you want me too
      Much as I'm wanting you
      Because wherever I am and whatever I do
      I want to be with you.

BARB McDONALD - I

The Broken Window

Love Crosses Borders

In the year 1865, the Hamilton family lived on a large plantation named Pleasant Hill, situated at the eastern end of the island in the parish of St. Thomas. Pleasant Hill was a large property of about 1,000 acres of sugarcane and banana cultivation.

The Hamilton family owned many slaves. These slaves lived in the barracks provided by the estate and they toiled in the fields from dawn to dusk. They were supervised by an overseer who rode a horse and carried a whip, which he used at the slightest infraction.

The Hamilton family lived in the great house. The family consisted of John and Fiona, his wife, and two small children. Robert, the eldest, was four years old and Chloe, his sister, just a babe in arms. The children had a nanny named Mildred.

Mildred was a slave woman from the estate who lived in the house with the family and who slept in a small room provided for her in the nursery suite. She had come to live in the house days after Robert's birth and had developed strong maternal feelings toward the children in her care.

John and Fiona had a very busy social life. They attended parties and picnics on the neighbouring plantations and even visited Kingston from time to time. A visit to Kingston took them away from home for days at a time; this was the horse and buggy era, and 70 miles was a long way to travel. The children spent most of their time with their nanny and they loved her dearly.

In 1865, in this area of St. Thomas, there was great unrest among the slaves. Conditions in both their living quarters and the fields where they worked were poor. The majority of the estate owners turned a blind eye to what was taking place in the barracks.

Mildred, of course, being a slave herself, was only too aware of the mutterings and sullen looks of her fellow slaves; she soon realized that the slaves were planning an uprising. The drums beat from dusk to dawn, sending messages to neighbouring estates about plans for the rebellion.

Mildred hated being a slave, but she loved the children in her care, she was sore at heart when she heard the details of the plot- all the estate owners and their families were to be killed. On the chosen day, the slaves were to wait for darkness to fall, then they would break into the houses while everyone was sleeping and murder the occupants with their machetes and seize the property for themselves. This was not a very brilliant plan because the British had a large garrison of troops stationed at Port Royal, but short term, it would be a blood bath.

Mildred made a plan of her own - she shared her plan with no one. On the night of the rebellion, she got the children ready for bed as usual. When dinner had been served and the house slaves had gone to their quarters, she wrapped a stone in a sock and broke the nursery room window. Outside in the shrubbery, she had hidden a donkey with two large wicker hampers, one hanging on each side of the donkey. This would attract no undue attention as these hampers were used to carry crops.

She quickly got the two sleepy children out of the window and into the garden. Robert thought it was a most exciting game, Chloe was not so sure, but with a piece of sugarcane to suck on, she soon settled in her hamper and fell asleep.

Mildred led the donkey out of the garden and through the fields, keeping well away from the main areas. She headed for the Blue Mountains where she hoped to meet with the Maroons, a bunch of fierce runaway slaves, who were a thorn in the side of the British troops. They travelled all night, the children were tired and hungry but she pressed on, trying to put as many miles as possible between Pleasant Hill and her motley little crew.

The terrain was rough and soon they were climbing steeply up a narrow rocky track. Day was dawning, soon she would have to find water and a place to rest.

They came to a clearing with a small stream and here they rested. Suddenly, Mildred realized they were not alone. She could feel the presence of many people, she was afraid, but she said, "Please help us, we come in peace and need your help."

The clearing suddenly filled with young men, who materialised out of the vegetation like ghosts out of the mist. One young man, who appeared to be the leader spoke, "Who are you, and what do you want? We are the Maroons, the runaway slaves who have made our home in these mountains. The British have put a bounty on our heads, so we are suspicious of visitors to our territory."

Mildred answered, "We come in peace and to beg for asylum. We cannot return to our home, for we will surely be killed."

The young men led Mildred and her charges into Accompong, the maroon town and into the house of their Chief. He was a tall good-looking man with a regal bearing. He listened carefully to Mildred's story then said, "You are welcome in Accompong but you cannot ever leave us. You are now Maroons, and I will be your Protector."

The rebellion was put down by the British in a most brutal manner. The leaders were hung in the square at Morant Bay. Today, in that Square stands a large statue of Paul Bogle, one of the leaders of the rebellion, who died by hanging at this spot. He is now considered a true Jamaican hero. Such is life!

BARB McDONALD - II

Silver Sands And Binoculars

On the north coast of Jamaica, about halfway between Ocho Rios and Montego Bay, lies the small town of Rio Bueno. The name of the town has never been Anglicised, and by the look of the few buildings on Main Street, nothing has changed since the Spanish were the rulers in Jamaica.

Just a mile or so more, and we make a sharp right turn into a small private road and drive towards the sea which is visible in the distance. Soon, we are at the main gate of Silver Sands, a community of holiday villas, some modest and others rather pretentious. There are no hotels or shops to mar the beauty of this special place. There is just a magnificent stretch of white sand and the deep blue ocean.

My aunt and uncle owned a villa here, they called the house Santa Margareta, I do not know why! The house was built on a bluff overlooking the ocean and the view from the deck was beyond compare. The walk down to the small beach was very steep, but my uncle, who was a very ingenious man, built steps all the way down. The steps went across the hill at an angle instead of straight down. This made it easier for the very young and the older folk to get down to the beach to swim.

My uncle often told us that he had wanted to be an engineer, but his father had insisted on keeping the family tradition and he had become a lawyer instead. All through his life, whenever he had time from a very busy schedule, he would work with his hands, roofing, plumbing, mason work and he seemed at peace doing manual labour.

The large window in the living area looked out on a panoramic view of the ocean in front and the beaches and houses nestled below. On a table, by the window, he kept a pair of powerful binoculars and a large log book.

Whenever he was at Santa Margareta, he spent many hours

studying everything he could see with his binoculars and entering the data in his log book. He left a note for his guests encouraging them to do the same.

My uncle told us that at 6:00 am, every morning, a large shark, which he had named Oscar, swam through the break in the reef. He would swim lazily around for a while and then return to the open sea. Sometimes, he even brought his family members for a visit.

At 3:00 pm, the shark would return and repeat his ritual. My uncle also kept track of the fishermen who sailed out before dawn for the early morning catch. As soon as he sighted the returning canoes, he would tell the cook to go down to the beach so she could have the first choice of snappers and lobsters.

His log held a detailed account of all the shipping that passed by, far beyond the reef. He could only see the details with his binoculars, of course.

There were large cruise ships, tankers, ore carriers and scruffy cargo vessels. When our children were young, we spent two glorious weeks each summer at this house. We carefully carried out my uncle's tradition, taking turns to watch the happenings in the ocean.

Many of his neighbors thought my uncle rather odd. The rumour was that he also spied on his neighbors, and kept a written inventory of the happenings in the houses around; I do not for a moment believe this gossip. Holiday places are often rife with gossip and wild behavior.

I am sure the Chief Justice of Jamaica would never stoop so low but then, lawyers have a reputation of being cagey and astute. I guess that once they ascend the bench and don the wig and gown, they put such temptations aside.

Santa Margareta now has a new owner. Sir Herbert went to his eternal rest many years ago. Whenever I visit Silver Sands, as I do most years, I always walk by the house that holds memories so dear to me. I wonder if anyone looks out to the sea with binoculars, and I wonder if Oscar's descendents still visit those beautiful waters.

BARB McDONALD - III

Behind The Wire

I met the Rhodes family when I was very young; they owned a large estate which joined my grandfather's land on one side. Major Rhodes was an absentee landlord; he visited Green Castle for about three months of the year and he had a resident manager. The Jamaican farmers who lived and worked on the farms in the area thought the Rhodes family rather pretentious. 'Hoity Toity', was the description often used.

The major came from very old English stock, Cecil Rhodes and the South African bunch and his wife Margaret was the daughter of the Governor of Vermont; they had one son whom they named John. The major was ex-Eaton and Sandhurst, and his son followed the family tradition and had joined his first regiment, "The Black Watch" just before the onset of the second world war. He was taken prisoner at Dunkirk, and remained in the camps for the next five years.

He and his friends tried to escape many times and eventually he ended up at Colditz Castle, that impregnable fortress the Germans thought to be escape proof and which they reserved for the most troublesome prisoners. I met John for the first time after the war in Europe ended. He had resigned his commission in the army and come to live in Jamaica at his father's farm. He loafed around, drove fast cars and did nothing much as far as the neighbors could tell, except drink and party rather too much. His father never forgave him for leaving the army; he never spoke another word to his son for as long as he lived.

Sometimes, on a Saturday evening, the guys would sit around drinking beer and shoot the breeze. On one such evening, I heard him talk briefly about his time in the camps. Just short acid remarks that gave me some idea at how very damaged he had been by his war.

"It was the sheer paralyzing boredom of it all, every day the same, and we never had enough to eat. There was the wire all around, it was never dark because of the search lights and the guards with the guns and the dogs on constant patrols... I hate Dobermans and German Shepherds," and then again, "I have seen friends of mine die trying to get through that wire." He would shudder and sip his drink.

He appeared to be a man who lived in the moment, without a care for the future or the past, but underneath this brash exterior he had a kind heart.

When my father passed away at the age of 49, John became a tower of strength to my mother. He taught her to drive and showed my young brother how to keep the estate books. My mother has never forgotten him. She had been very unprepared for widowhood. Married at eighteen, with four children and living a rather isolated life in the country, she had depended on my father for everything. I know John set her on the path to becoming self-sufficient and eventually running a thriving flower-growing operation.

John never really settled into civilian life; he never planned for his future. What happened just happened and he dealt with events as they unfolded.

He married three times and had five children. I think the women in his life found it impossible to understand his philosophy on life and they just got discouraged and walked away. His two sons followed the family tradition, went into the British Army and fought in various countries of the world. I correspond with Fiona, his eldest daughter; we exchange Christmas letters and I get the update on family news.

John died ten years ago. His was a sad life in many ways, at least I think so. A bright handsome young man in the prime of his life, so much unfulfilled promise. His years behind the fences damaged him greatly. I guess he was one of many young men who suffered this fate.

EILEEN SLEATH - I

My Achilles' Heel

I remember crossing the Irish Sea when I was about eleven years of age. What a motley crew we were, my three brothers and I, travelling alone. I was supposed to mother them, but was being violently sick every five minutes. Drowning was looking more and more attractive: it was horrible, never again!

Going across the sea to Ireland did not affect me, but going home again to England certainly did: bad memories.

Last night, I took a special tour to Ireland - I FLEW into Dublin! As my mother loved that city, she was the one I chose to show me the sights. Good move! We had a wonderful time - Guinness was too heavy tasting for me, but we got drunk on the music and songs in the pubs, swept along on the "live for today" attitude of the Irish. Mother and I held hands, close, and we looked at all the places I had dreamed about for years.

Stopping to kiss the Blarney Stone in Cork was a must. I had read so much about the mind-boggling history of Blarney Castle, I didn't need a guide.

Next stop was County Meath, where mother was born. My brothers and I spent time there as children, so I remembered it with a child's eye: looking along the boreen in Balivor (*boreen* is a narrow, frequently unpaved, rural road in Ireland), I could see three dirty little kids, trying to find where the chickens had laid their eggs - lucky, lucky me, to see it all again.

Ireland is filled with fairy folklore, tales of little people, and ghosts are part of life. It happened to be Halloween, so off to the graveyard I went and met my grandparents, aunts, uncles and cousins. They were all waiting for me as if they knew I was coming and everybody talked to one another - it felt like a party. Mother smiled at me. What a wonderful morning - I don't remember ever feeling so relaxed. My dreams last night were wonderful. Ireland - I will never close my mind to it again.

EILEEN SLEATH - II

Life Changes

Patricia sat on her deck, alone, watching the sunrise. The summer so far had matched her life - wet, miserable, uncertain. She didn't enjoy being at the cottage.

The view of the lake and the mainland were spectacular, the water so calm and smooth you'd swear you could skate on it. There were a few eager fishermen already out and some cheerfully waved at her; she managed a half-hearted wave back.

And then she saw them, a family of ducks. She watched for several minutes as mother and father ducks were kept busy keeping their babies in straight lines as they swam by.

Of course, there were one or two of the ducklings that seemed hell bent on going their own way; and Patricia chuckled. It was then it happened: she felt every bone in her body relax, and a cloak of calmness wrap itself around her.

For years, she'd stressed at the to-ing and fro-ing to this place: the gathering of children and food, the long over-familiar drive, with her voice being the only dissenting one. And yet every visitor to the cottage had called it Paradise - perhaps, after all, they were right.

No one else was up, so she sat on in this mellow mood. Was it then that she'd dozed off? How else to explain the unexplainable, the ghosts taking over her mind. And there were so many of them; people she'd loved but were no longer with her, but somehow all of them there, standing on the beach talking to her. Some were family members, others much loved friends, and they all had the same message: *GET ON WITH YOUR LIFE!*

You have so much love left to give, be happy, share it! Stop crying for us, just remember the happy times we shared.

Patricia felt completely disoriented: something was pulling at her robe. "Mamma, I'm hungry and you're the only one awake. I want my breakfast."

"Okay little boy, do you like pancakes?"

"My favourite. I love you."

EILEEN SLEATH - III

Lost Childhood

November arrives so quickly, most of us start thinking that Christmas is just around the corner and saying what happened to summer? I don't like November!

Yet, as a child it was an exciting month. Knowing why I find that it's a sad month doesn't help.

Remembrance Day, November 11th. In the old days we called it Armistice Day. My father told us that the people were honouring all the men who died or were injured in the war.

We had no concept of war; we just enjoyed the bands and the marching soldiers.

My big brother was a cadet, so he was dressed in his uniform, marching with the other boys. The pipes and drums were the best. I loved watching them and listening to the music.

Mother had to hold my hand tightly to stop me from following the bands. The marching soldiers got the most cheers and I noticed with pride that my father, who marched with them, was the tallest and the most handsome.

Things changed; war was declared and we soon found out what that meant. Children in those days were seen but not heard. We were removed from our homes to live with strangers. Nobody told us why. Even being told it was to keep us safe didn't convince us that it was the right thing to happen.

Our father and big brother appeared dressed in marching uniforms and left home. We clung together and spoke in whispers. Yes! We soon found out what being at war meant.

My father never did come home. They sent my mother a telegram telling her he was missing, believed killed. I spent a lot of years looking for him to come back. Maybe he had just lost his memory.

Remembrance Day was observed at the Cenotaph in Ottawa last week and I viewed it all day.

The pipes and drums were wonderful. The pipers wearing their kilts are always my favourite.

Hearing the bugler play the last post allows me to cry enough tears for the year.

I really think though that most of the tears were for a little girl who lost her daddy.

Journey Through Life

Amazing how a word, smell and, sometimes a particular tune, can transport you to another place and time.

We are inundated at this time of year with television pictures of the war and the men who fought in it.

Remembrance Day, November 11th. I watched the service on the television, the veterans all looked so proud, but we see fewer of them every year.

In my mind, I became the same bewildered little girl I was when the war started.

Our world was changing but nobody was telling us why.

September 3rd 1939 will always stay in my memory. Our parents were listening to the radio we heard our father say: "This is it. We are at war."

The most upsetting thing for us four children, was our mother crying.

"Fred, you can't go, we need you."

"You will make out okay, you'll have the children."

"Life will never be the same again."

The two boys held my hands and we went off to our fort. The kid brother was walking by this time, so we let him come with us.

The house where we lived had a gate at the end of the garden, it opened up to a huge bank that ran down to train tracks. We were threatened with house arrest if we ever ventured out there. Our father fixed up seating for us to watch the trains go by.

We talked and tried to make sense of what was happening; we couldn't, so we played...

It took us years to understand the repercussions of war. Father never came back. We played together, went to school, missed our father but mother was always there. Most of all, we had each other. But mother was right, life was never the same.

I never mind being transported back to the life I had with my brothers and our fort. I find it very comforting.

CAROL RAYMOND - I

Escape

Jim only allowed Lorraine to go to a few places by herself. She could go to the grocery store, she could do her shifts at the restaurant and she could go to church on Sunday. The church ladies had been begging her to come to help with some of their outreach projects and she was running out of reasons to decline. Finally, Jim said she could go to help them on Wednesday afternoons, probably just so that they would stop calling all the time. He did not like to be disturbed.

Lorraine had never been in any kind of trouble. Even when she was still in high school she never missed a class or handed in an assignment late. When the other kids were at parties drinking and experimenting with drugs, she was at home watching TV or babysitting for her neighbour Tricia. Tricia was only four years older than her, but already had a little boy and seemed to know so much more about the world. It was actually at Tricia's house that it all started. Tricia's brother, Jim, sometimes came around and he and Lorraine became good friends. Although he was a few years older than her, he was attentive and made her feel very special.

Nobody was happy when they decided to marry. Lorraine's parents thought she was too young and Tricia looked very worried. After the wedding, they moved to a small town about 200 kilometres away. Lorraine was very happy at first. Nobody here knew what a loser she had been in high school; she had a handsome husband and felt like she finally belonged somewhere.

It didn't take long for things to unravel. Jim drank a lot and became more and more possessive. It was only when his hours were drastically cut at the plant that he agreed to allow her to look for a job. The restaurant was old and a bit dingy, but served a steady clientele of locals and people just passing through town.

Lorraine loved the work; at least, she loved meeting the people she waited on. Her co-workers were friendly, but she kept her distance from them. Jim did not want her to socialise. She was to be available to him at all times.

The first time he hit her, she really wasn't all that shocked. She had almost been expecting it. That night she was an hour late getting home from work as the guy who normally did the cleanup had called in sick.

After that, the beatings happened more and more frequently. Before long, the regular customers began to notice her carefully disguised bruises and she knew they did not believe her stories of falls and accidents. Some of them tried to give her information about shelters, but she always denied there was a problem and couldn't figure out how she would even get to one of those places. She thought of reporting the abuse to the police, but whenever she imagined the rage she would face at home, she shivered and put that thought out of her mind.

Jim drove her to the church on Wednesday afternoon and told her he would be back to get her in exactly two hours. She knew he would spend most of the time sitting in the car in the parking lot just watching and waiting.

She liked the work here, though. Opening the bags of donated clothing and deciding what to do with it seemed to give her life some purpose. Sometimes, the items went directly to needy families in the community, other times they were donated to local charities. She worked quickly and methodically and without thinking too much about the shambles her life was in.

Suddenly, her sense of peace was shattered as she felt something strange at the bottom of the bag she was unpacking. For some reason she looked around and made sure that nobody else was watching before she lifted out a small shoebox, carefully sealed with duct tape and elastic bands.

With shock, she realized that there was an envelope attached to the box with her name on it. As her heart pounded and her body shook she tore the envelope open. The short note said only, "For you - just in case". She was almost numb with fear as she wondered what she would find and who knew she was going to be there that afternoon.

Carefully, she opened the box and stared at a small, black revolver.

With her heart racing and feeling as if she might pass out, she placed the gun in her handbag and put the instructions that accompanied it in the back pocket of her jeans. There was no time to figure out the meaning of all this right now, but she suddenly realised that she might have options after all.

When the other women came back from their coffee break, she smiled at them and chatted. They were surprised at her sudden friendliness and ecstatic that their good deeds had finally helped her come out of her shell.

As Lorraine walked to the car to meet Jim she held her bag carefully and forced herself to answer his probing questions. The time was not right yet but it was coming soon. It was coming soon and she was going to be ready.

CAROL RAYMOND - II

Take-A-Way

The dirty, cracked wooden sign was barely visible through the thick growth of trees and shrubs by the side of the road. In the many years Phil had been driving to his remote fishing cabin he had never seen any signs of life here. There were never any people or vehicles, no dogs barking or music playing. As the welcome transition to a stress free environment beckoned, he did wonder fleetingly about the meaning of the strange words on the sign, "Take-A-Way", and wondered what might really be back there.

Today might be the day he found out. As he approached the steep hill where the rustic, weathered sign appeared, his car was sputtering and unresponsive. Although he pushed hard on the accelerator, it drifted to a stop and a puff of thick, black smoke wafted out from under the hood.

Phil and his friends, Jake and Tom, sat quietly for a few seconds before the cursing started. Tom flung the hood open and fiddled under it for a few minutes. However, the truth was that they were all Bay Street bankers who paid mechanics to look after their cars and none of them had the slightest idea what was wrong, let alone how to fix it. All of them reached into their pockets and pulled out their cell phones but there was simply no reception in this forlorn place. For these men, used to being in charge and in control, there was a gnawing feeling of fear.

Pulling their jackets around them to fend off the damp, cool air, they looked around at the thick forests on each side of the road and listened to the eerie silence. Other than the occasional crackling of a branch or a bird's chirp there were no sounds.

Against all odds they talked about whether the inhabitants of "Take-A-Way" might have a vehicle they could borrow. Tentatively, the three pushed their way along an old winding path under the sign until they came to a fork with two arrows pointing in different directions. Although there were no words, the arrows seemed to be taunting them to "take a way". After a few minutes of arguing they tossed a coin and trudged off on the path to the left.

As they continued the path became narrower and more overgrown. Within a half hour they had arrived at an old fire pit. It did not appear to have been used in several years and there was nothing to indicate that any form of civilization was near.

With increasing fear and the spectre of darkness arriving within a few hours, the three quickly retraced their steps. There was no talking now - only a feeling of dread as they realized they might really be in trouble.

When they reached the arrows, they immediately started off along the second path. Each of them felt a tiny glimmer of hope that help would be waiting for them at the end of the trail, but they were smart, realistic men and they knew the odds were not good. This path was even more overgrown than the last one and it certainly appeared that nobody had used it for a very long time.

They stoically plodded along, brushing away the prickly pine boughs and random limbs of old trees and shrubs. Although the conversation had stopped, each of them knew they were not alone in wondering if the time had come to return to the disabled car and wait for help there.

At long last, the path began to widen and shards of sunlight began to filter through the overhead canopy. And suddenly there it was. A small cabin sat in a tiny clearing. As they approached, no sign of human existence was evident but it seemed to be well maintained. When there was no response to their knocks or yells, they tried to open the door and to their shock the unlocked door opened on the first try.

Inside they found cooking implements, matches, blankets, sleeping bags, rainwear and shelves full of canned goods. On the floor sat a huge container of water. Through the window they caught glimpses of the lake below.

Although they felt like intruders and wondered how the owner would react if he returned, they knew that for their safety they would have to stay the night. As the late afternoon light filtered in to the room their attention was grabbed by a small glass ornament on a table that was reflecting the soft light. Phil found himself being drawn to it and was startled to find a neatly printed note sitting at its base. He read aloud to the others who gathered near.

"Welcome, visitors to Take-A-Way. If you are here, you must be needing help. Please take whatever you need to be comfortable. I have to go away but am happy to share my special place with you. I only ask that you leave something behind so that the next person who comes by will be all right too." It was signed by someone called Sam.

After a good night of sleep, the three made use of a sturdy rowboat they found hidden by the shore and were able to reach the small town where they had started their journey around the lake. In town, they spent the morning trying to find Sam so that they could repay him. The truth was even stranger than their journey had been.

The townspeople knew Sam but were very clear that he had died in the town hospital after arriving very ill at least ten years ago. His place had been called "Take-A-Way", but it had been razed in a fire shortly after his death. He had no family and the cabin was long gone.

After paying one of the men in town to take them back and fix the car, the three convinced him to hike with them to the cabin to prove it was still there. This time they moved along the path with enthusiasm. As they approached the clearing they saw a pile of old ashes, some pieces of blackened lumber and the strange glass ornament. As the town mechanic shook his head and returned to the car, they sat dazed on the ground.

Before they started back to the trail, each of the men took something from his back pack and placed it gently on the ground beside the ornament. In silence, the three walked back to the road knowing that something big had happened here and that their lives would never be the same again.

CAROL RAYMOND - III

The Good Deal

Jim fought feelings of hopelessness as he made his final stop of the day. He desperately needed a new car and, so far, the only things in his price range looked like they might have a life span of about a week.

Although he had been warned about the small dealers along this sleazy strip of rundown establishments, he really had no other choice but to see what they could offer. He did know a thing or two about cars and was confident he would be able to spot any major issues.

The salesman, Rex, listened to his predicament with obviously fake enthusiasm and shook his head when he heard how much Jim was able to spend. He led him to look at a couple of cars at the back of the lot but the bodies were in such disrepair that Jim did not even bother taking either of them out for a test drive.

Rex cleared his throat loudly and with carefully measured consideration took Jim to a grey, metallic compact car that didn't seem to be more than five years old. The hours that Jim had spent looking on line, in auto trade magazines and at various dealers left no doubt in his mind that the fair price for this car would be well above what he could pay.

"Let's take it for a drive," Rex suggested, his voice booming as he slapped Jim on the shoulders.

Jim was excited but a bit annoyed at the same time. With work and school, he really didn't have time for joy rides - and yet he guessed that there would be no harm in trying it out. He couldn't even remember when he had last gone for a drive without worrying that his car would break down or a malfunction would cause an accident.

It drove like a dream. It stopped smoothly at red lights and felt powerful on the highway. As they returned to the small trailer that served as an office, Jim savoured the satisfied feeling that he knew would be short lived. "I won't keep you in suspense Jim," Rex said. "Did you like the car?"

"Of course, I loved it," responded Jim with thinly veiled sarcasm evident in his wistful voice.

"Well, you seem like a great guy and I would really like for you to have it. I think we can work something out."

When the final price was shown to Jim, he could barely breath. He was shocked to realise that he could actually afford this car. However, determined not to be taken advantage of, he brought a mechanic to look at it and did a search to see if it had ever been involved in an accident.

Surprisingly, everything appeared to be in order and he started to feel a little giddy. As he waited for the paper work to be completed, Jim was more impatient than he ever remembered feeling. He just couldn't wait to get the car out on the road and was afraid the deal would be somehow scrapped even before it was completed.

Finally back behind the wheel, Jim adjusted the side mirrors and the rear view mirror. As he fiddled with the rear view mirror at a stop sign he seemed to catch a fleeting glimpse of something unusual. "It must be the way the light is reflecting," Jim thought. He determined that he would look at it again in the daylight.

The next day, the same thing happened. Jim didn't want to believe there was a problem, so he ignored it again. However, eventually he had to admit that there was something odd occurring.

Each time he looked in the rear view mirror, he could see the face of a very sad man looking back at him. He assumed it must be some kind of optical illusion and was determined to find out what was causing it. Unfortunately, it soon became clear that it didn't matter how he moved the mirror, how he adjusted the seat, what time of day it was, whether it was sunny or cloudy - no matter where he went, the sad man went with him. Before long, it was not just the image in the mirror but also the presence of the man that he felt.

With great dismay, Jim returned to the somewhat sketchy dealer and explained that he wanted to return the car. To his surprise, he realised that Rex seemed to have been almost expecting it.

"Do you mind explaining the reason you're bringing it back?" Rex asked quietly.

"Well," explained Jim sheepishly, "it sounds crazy but every time I look in the rear view mirror I see the face of a man looking back at me." Jim stammered with embarrassment as he continued, "The thing is that I always feel like there is someone else in the car with me."

Jim knew how all of this must sound and he knew that Rex was under no obligation to take the car back.

He felt his face turn red and he suddenly felt very hot. He looked at the floor for a few minutes before he had the nerve to look up. When he finally raised his eyes, he was shocked to see that Rex was not laughing or smiling with pity. In fact, Rex looked even shakier than he did. His ruddy complexion had turned ashen and the boisterous confidence was gone.

Quietly, he told Jim that he was the third person who had returned the car and each of them had told exactly the same story. After the second person brought the car back, Rex had done some investigation of his own. It seemed that the original owner had left the car unlocked one bitterly cold winter night.

The next morning the body of a homeless man was found sitting in the back seat.

Rex looked grave as he wrote a cheque to Jim for the full amount he had paid. As Jim left the trailer, Rex was sitting with his head in his hands. "I won't sell this car again," he said to no one in particular. "I won't sell it again."

JOY ENGLAND - I

Calligraphy

I hop off the bus and I'm ambling along the sidewalk when suddenly it hits me – the brainwave, genius idea, cunning plan, whatever - I'll go to night school, take an evening class and improve myself. That should please the old man.

He's always dropping heavy hints about me upgrading my education and "making something of myself ". I did graduate from high school, just, but college didn't seem to call out to me in a meaningful way back then, and I've drifted along, in and out of jobs ever since, getting nowhere fast, I suppose.

Don't get me wrong. I'm happy enough, well, as happy as a 25 year old guy can be, living in his parents' basement (good home-cooked meals, comfy bed, washing done by doting mother), working as a shelf-stocker and general dogsbody at our local Sobey's and hanging out with a bunch of pals at the snooker hall in the evening. Not exactly the high life, I have to admit, and lately, I've felt unsettled somehow and even more unfocussed than usual. So, night class it is. I'm about to discover myself, at last.

Maybe?

At home, I browse through the Fall brochures from the nearest community college, both boards of education and the city's parks and recreation department. Wow! So much to do! So little time!

Seriously, it blows my mind the number of classes and courses out there. How do people find the time to eat and sleep, let alone go to work? Beer in hand, I settle down to study everything on offer in the hope that something will really grab me.

Ballroom dancing? No. Fusion yoga? Hardly! Calculus? No way! Oh my god! I flip through the pages in a panic. This is harder than I expected, then, tucked away at the bottom of a page the word Calligraphy leaps out at me. I read the tiny blurb describing the course, which doesn't tell me much, but I have a gut feeling that this is the one for me. Never mind that I hardly know what calligraphy is. This course is calling out to me. The parents, when informed of my decision to sign up for calligraphy, seem less enthusiastic than I'd hoped for, especially Dad.

"What good will that do you?" he asks, a frown on his face.

I don't have a ready answer for him but Mum pipes up, "You never know where these things will lead, Al."

She's great at sticking up for me. She's had lots of practice.

Two weeks later, on a Thursday night, off I go to my first class. I feel good. I know this is going to change my life! I'll learn how to be a master calligrapher, if that's the word, and people will pay big bucks to have me hand-write their special invitations in looped, cursive writing, and in no time I'll be able to afford my own pad, a loft apartment down town, close to the action, and away from Dad's disapproving glare. Gorgeous women will compete for my attention and I'll be spoilt for choice. Bring it on!

What can I say? It doesn't turn out exactly the way I'd planned. The teacher's nice, a pleasant middle-aged woman, very encouraging, but not really dynamic. The other students are also nice; a mixed bunch of married ladies, who talk about their offspring all the time, an artsy guy with a straggly beard and even wilder artistic ambitions than mine (crazy!), and Anica.

On the first evening I hardly notice her. She's one of those small, quiet girls and she works away at her lettering and doesn't talk to anyone. During the second class, Mrs. Thing, the teacher, holds up Anica's paper as an example to the rest of us, noting her "careful downstrokes" and "meticulous spacing". Her efforts are certainly better than any one else's but, frankly, what impresses me is her long, dark hair, big brown eyes and petite, but shapely, figure. I manage to sidle up to her during coffee break and engage her in conversation. She has a charming accent I can't quite place and a lovely smile. Boy! I'm smitten!

Of course, I keep on with the calligraphy class for a few more sessions so I can get to know Anica better. Turns out she's from Croatia and has only been in Canada for a couple of years. Her English is really good. I'm impressed. We are now, as they say, an item. She is a great girl and, strangely enough, she loves me! Even though the calligraphy hasn't turned out to be my way to fortune and fame, it has certainly changed my life.

My next evening classes are going to be in the business and management field. Anica and I hope to get married next year. I'll need a real job so that we can have a good life together. Who'd have thought fancy writing could make such a difference in a person's life? I suppose I have my grumpy Dad to thank for this. He's the one who kept telling me to change my outlook on life and look to the future. So I have and the future is rosy!

JOY ENGLAND - II

Coffee Time

"Can I help you?" the bored voice of the young girl broke in on Angela's reverie.

"Oh, yes, just a regular coffee, please, and a tea biscuit."

She carried her tray to a table in the far corner of the busy coffee shop and sat in a spot where she could see the whole room and yet be inconspicuous. What on earth am I doing here? She wondered. She was not in the habit of spending time alone drinking coffee and eating fattening snacks in cafes, but today was different. Somehow she had to get through it, and if that meant wasting time buying things she didn't need just to postpone going home to that empty house, well, so be it.

It's quite noisy in here, she thought. What's everyone talking about so animatedly? At the next table three young girls were huddled together over their drinks and doughnuts, giggling and gasping over the exploits of a friend, perhaps.

"She went to his place after the dance?"

"Yeah, she told me!"

"What happened then?"

Angela turned away, not wishing to hear further details of this teenage drama.

It seemed light years away from the life she was leading now, not surprisingly, considering that today was her fiftieth birthday. She felt so elderly, and it was raining, too.

"Is anyone sitting here?" A tall man gestured towards the chair opposite her with his rolled umbrella, and placed his coffee down on the table when she shook her head in answer. He dragged the chair out noisily and sat down with much arranging of his raincoat and newspaper.

'I hope I'm not disturbing you," he said, "but there weren't any other seats left and I had to get in out of this rain."

Please, I'm not in the mood for idle conversation, Angela groaned inwardly, but managed an inane comment about the awful weather, along with a polite smile.

They sipped their coffees and sat quietly for a moment or two trying to avoid making eye contact, which was rather difficult when they were sitting directly opposite one another.

"Haven't I seen...?"

"Are you in the...?"

They both spoke at once and stopped suddenly, embarrassed, then Angela began again.

"You belong to the photography group down at the college, don't you?

"Yes, that's where I've seen you," he laughed. "I knew you looked familiar."

He introduced himself. "Tom Williams, retired teacher" and, in no time, it seemed, they were chatting away like old friends. Half an hour flew by and it was time to go. Angela stood up, gathered her scarf and gloves and prepared to leave. She smiled at Tom.

"It's been nice talking to you."

He got up, and looked directly at her.

"And you, too. We must do this again, if you'd like to, only perhaps dinner would be better. More time to talk!"

"That would be lovely," Angela smiled again. "I'll give you my phone number, shall I?"

JOY ENGLAND - III

Long Distance

The phone rang, loud and shrill in the empty hall. No one came to answer it. The afternoon sun shone through the high window and specks of dust stirred lazily in the warm air. Everyone was outside, working in the garden or down on the promenade enjoying the sea breezes. Suddenly, the phone burst into life again, even more urgently, it seemed, and this time, Betty, who had just popped out to the shop for an ice cream cone, heard it and raced through the front door, grabbing the receiver off the wall.

"Douglas 439!" she yelled, out of breath.

"I have a long distance call for you from Halifax, Yorkshire. Please hold." The dulcet tones of the operator echoed down the line.

Betty gasped. Perhaps it was news about Tom, her brother-in law. It was three days after Dunkirk and, so far, they had heard nothing. Had he been amongst the thousands who had been rescued from the beaches or had he been taken prisoner by the Germans and was, even now, en route to a prison camp? They didn't dare think about the third possibility.

Still clutching the phone close to her ear, Betty leaned out of the window and shouted as loudly as she could,

"Jean, Jean, come to the phone! Quick! I think Tom's trying to reach you!"

Her sister, busy picking carnations for a wedding bouquet at the far side of the garden, heard the shouts and dropped the flowers where she stood. Her heart pounding, she ran through the flower bed, around the side of the house and in at the door, taking the phone from Betty's outstretched hand, all in a matter of seconds.

"Yes? Hello? Tom?"

"One moment, caller." The operator's voice sounded faint. "I'll connect you now."

There was a crackling noise and some odd-sounding clicks and then, quietly but clearly, Jean heard the voice she knew so well.

"Jean, it's me, Tom. I'm OK. I got out and I'm in Yorkshire. I can't talk long. There's a queue of fellows waiting but I'll try again..."

The phone went dead. Jean sat down on the bench beneath the phone, her legs suddenly weak.

"Thank God," she whispered; and wept for joy.

Family Doctor

She sits slumped in her ergonomically designed chair and gazes out of the window, a thoughtful expression on her face. It's her lunch break and today she has a whole half-hour in which to eat, because it's also her turn to take the walk-in clinic later this afternoon. That means she'll be lucky if she gets home before nine tonight. She sees the traffic rushing along the busy city street below her and wonders where everyone is going so fast. Her life at present seems hemmed in by the four walls of the medical building and her home a few miles away on the outskirts of town.

She turns away from the window suddenly and looks down at her desk. Nothing too exciting there; a computer screen ready for her to enter details of her patients' ailments, a box of tissues, a couple of medical files she really ought to glance at and her fountain pen. What did she expect? In ten minutes or so, her first patient of the afternoon will be ushered in. Kate Gardener, a pleasant woman in her mid-fifties, who usually comes by every few weeks just to make sure that her minor problems are still minor. They have a pleasant chat, a prescription is written, if necessary, and Kate goes on her way, reassured for another month or two.

"And I stay here, trapped in this small, white room with nothing to liven it up apart from the two Group of Seven prints on the wall and the photograph of Mikey on the desk. I should get a tiger skin rug!"

She laughs at her own silliness, then she picks up the picture of her small son, smiling at his sweet, chubby face and big brown eyes. He's such a treasure. She really should be at home with him, taking care of him, going to the swings in the park and making him special lunches. And yet, when she thinks of all those years of training and the difference her knowledge and skills can make to her patients' lives, she knows that she is in the right place, at least for now.

Around her, she hears the sounds of a busy practice, footsteps in the hallway outside her room, the booming baritone of her colleague, Fred McAllister, in the next office and the muted ring of the telephone in the reception area. Then there's the sound of female voices outside her door, the nurse and Kate Gardener, she assumes. There's a light tap on the door and Kate enters, all smiles, and settles herself down on the chair. The doctor turns towards her, a professional, yet welcoming expression on her face.

"Hello, Kate, how are you today?"

This feels right. She's comfortable in this role. Her earlier discontent fades away as she listens to her patient tell of her aches and pains. She leans forward and pats her knee.

"I'm sure we can find something to help you with that," she says, turning to the computer to write up her notes.

DOROTHY COATES - I

Relief

The area was wild and desolate. Mabel knew though that trains did come through sometimes. The railway station was merely a hut on the platform of wood piling and did not offer much shelter. Mabel waited and waited with her two-year-old son clinging on to her skirt.

It was still dawn, the daylight barely showing through clouds which threatened rain.

Jimmy started to cry. "Is my daddy coming on the train wiv us?" he asked between sobs.

"No darling, not this time. We're going on a special train. Don't cry, you are mummy's big boy and big boys don't cry."

Meanwhile, Mabel was a little worried herself. Would Ted wake up and find them missing and come looking for them? Ted had been drinking heavily the night before. Maybe it would take a while to sleep it off, she hoped.

Mabel's bones ached from the pummelling she had taken and her face was swollen, making her eye feel almost closed.

The rain started falling, adding to Mabel's discomfort.

"Hush Jimmy, listen! Can you hear that whistle? That's the train. It won't be long now."

She picked her son up and hugged him.

The sound on the rumbling track came closer. It seemed slower than she thought and then it came in view. "Oh no," she said "it's a freight train." There has to be another train, life will not disappoint me, would it?

A signal siren coming close assailed her ears as two police cars came into view. Two policemen alighted, walked over to Mabel with guns drawn and one of them asked, "Are you alone? We are here to help you. You can go back home after you have been checked over at the hospital".

"My husband?" Mabel asked.

"He is safely in jail and is likely to be there for some time. Don't you worry Mrs. Tomkin, we have been onto him for sometime. Your neighbours reported the violence this morning. You may need to replace some of your furniture."

Turning to leave with the police, Mabel heard another train whistle. Should she leave the train station? With thoughts about the life ahead, Mabel and Jimmy got into the police car.

DOROTHY COATES - II

I Should've Said Goodbye

"Stop it! Don't! What did I do?" screamed Alice, raising her arms to shield her face from the blows of her husband's ham-like fists. Her head hit the wall. Thwack! Stars blinked before her eyes and bells echoed through her ears.

"You whore! You bitch!" He turned away, only to turn back again with a gun pulled from the drawer behind him. "Now, who was he?" Eric demanded, "Don't lie to me. It must have been important for you to get a neighbour to sit with the children."

Her body shaking in fear, Alice tried to answer between uncontrollable sobs, "I only went to meet Joan at..." She didn't get a chance to finish the sentence. Another blow, this time with the blunt end of the gun.

Morning found Alice struggling to open her eyes which were mere slits, the eyelids being so puffed. A glance in the mirror told the horrible story. The face peering back at her was bruised, the nose swollen twice its size. Wincing, she gently washed and patted it dry as Beth toddled into the bathroom to use the potty. Karen toddled in after her, rubbing sleep from her eyes. Eric had not yet left for work and could be within earshot.

"What did you do to your face, Mummy?"

"Mummy fell of her bike."

"Ooh, does it hurt? Can you see? Look Kawen, Mummy's got a fat face." Beth always had a hard time sounding her Rs.

"I'm fine, lovely, and yes, Mummy can see."

"Does Daddy know?"

"Yes, chatterbox, Daddy knows. Come here and let me wash your hands and face and then we can go down for breakfast." Alice picked up little Karen and downstairs they went.

"I've made tea," said Eric, turning to look at the trio as they entered. "You had better let the doctor take a look at you. I'll see you later," said Eric as he kissed the girls goodbye.

"Daddy didn't kiss you, Mummy," said Beth.

"He didn't want to hurt Mummy's nose," she answered. After breakfast, Alice asked her neighbour, Ivy, to watch the little ones while she went to the doctor.

Clouds of vapour crossed her vision as Alice felt herself drift in a sea of light. Pictures tumbled like a kaleidoscope in her brain; she felt warm and happy as one emerged. She was on the shore of a huge lake, surrounded by lush green hills. Eric was there. Arms outstretched, she ran to him and he picked her up.

They kissed and, laughing, fell down on the warm, sweet grass. The lay close, loving, their bodies caressed by the warm sun. He kissed her brow, pushing aside the curls. The gentle breeze blew wisps across her face.

A cloud crossed the sun. Everything went dark. The kaleidoscope turned and the scene changed. Her firstborn was in her arms. Beth was gurgling happily as her father splashed the tiny, unshod toes with water dripping from his tousled wet hair. Eric had just finished swimming six laps of the Olympic-sized pool just around the corner from where they had lived. Alice and he had often taken turns watching the baby while the other took to the water. Beth loved it, lying in her pram at the water's edge, being petted and spoiled by everyone who passed by.

Joy surged through her being as once again the kaleidoscope turned. She was in a hospital, her heart so full, it felt ready to burst. Eric kissed her while taking her and their second newborn in his embrace. Alice could smell the roses he was holding.

The perfume drifted past her nostrils again. Roses! Was this real? Alice tried to open her eyes, but it was too much of an effort. To just drift in the mists, amid a warm sea of love felt wonderful. She tried again. This time, through narrow slits, she saw them. Red and yellow blossoms, Her eyes focused on Eric, holding them, tears in his eyes. "I must still be dreaming."

"No, you are not dreaming," said Eric. "I'm here. You're just waking up from the anaesthetic and going to be fine. As soon as you can stand, I'll take you home." It had felt so nice to drift and dream. Alice hardly felt like standing up. She lifted her hand to feel the gauze bandage which almost covered her eyes as well and closed them, remembering. "It's alright, love, don't touch. I'll never hurt you again. I swear. How could I hurt your lovely face?"

Struggling to open her eyes again, she smiled. Her hubby was at her side, waiting to take her home. Everything would be alright now. Wouldn't it?

DOROTHY COATES - III

Sixth Sense

Do you ever think that a dream or just a feeling that something is going to happen and it does?

This happened to me. It was about a dream in which I was being beaten horribly and waking up suddenly, sweat on my brow and down my back. I said out loud, "Thank goodness, that it was only a dream, or was it a premonition."

It was whatever you would like to call it, because everything was happening just like I knew it would. I jumped out of bed and this probably saved my life.

He stood by the door, eyes burning like red hot coals, coming towards me; it looked like a knife in his hand, it turned out to be scissors, which this man threw at me. "Now you won't wear your fancy dresses any more, I will cut them up."

Eric, for that was his name, now came right into the room quickly and punched me on the chin; another blow caught me on the nose which started to bleed. This mad man then dragged me into the bathroom, telling me to wash my face which had started to swell.

Feeling sick to my stomach and very frightened, I suddenly remembered my dream. It had told me to leave the house by the back way, knowing it opened into a lane.

This I did, because I also remembered workmen came through the lane often and I could get a lift to the doctor or the police.

Trusting my instincts, I stood in the middle of the lane, raising my left hand with the other one still holding a hand towel to my nose.

Eventually, a white van came by and took me to the hospital. After waiting for some time, I was informed that my nose was broken and jaw cracked. It could have been worse had I not paid heed to my dream, my premonition.

CONTRIBUTORS

JEANETTE CLARKE
An avid reader of crime fiction who indulges in a little murder and mayhem in her own writing. Short stories published in the United Kingdom and the United States.

RICHARD TORPEY
Deceased. Always lively and expressive, Richard rose to the challenge when it came to his writing. He wrote many happy, intriguing and observant stories. He hoped his children would some day enjoy and remember him through his memoirs. His passing was a major loss for the Creative Writing Group.

KONRAD BRINCK
German-born immigrant who had a long career in sales and marketing. His soon-to-be-published memoirs 'It's Just Me' highlights his upbringing in post-war Berlin and his life with his South African-born wife Jacqueline and their daughter Toni.

MARGARET HOLLIWELL

Has always enjoyed writing and won second place in the Toronto Star's short story competition when it was launched in 1988. Then made aquaintance with the owner of the Highway Book Shop in Cobalt, that resulted in the publication of a 'health' book. Still writing and 'wanting to write till the end of time'.

DOUG GAYNOR

Has been an avid short story teller across all genres, from children's stories to murder mysteries and everything in between. Loves to see the humor in situations and write about them. Favorite travel is river boat cruising in Europe and elsewhere.

MARY SANDOR

Mother-grandmother-great grandmother. Published author of several short stories and political essays. Loves to write, is fond of music, travel and good books. Interested in interior decorating. Enjoys sun-filled days and appreciates good friends. Would like to find the meaning of life.

RENA FLANNIGAN

Chose to be a Canadian as a youngster; and has lived in Ontario since 1952. Tailoress, fur finisher, vice-principal of a private school, self-employed business owner, tour manager and guide, champion speed skater-tennis player-skier-ballroom and Latin dancing trophy winner. Now an author.

MARGARET CAREY

A retired health care worker, avid traveller, accomplished pianist, volunteer, wife, mother and grandmother. Co-author of a book on Medical Radiation Technology, as well as having entries of poetry in Young Canadian Writers' book. Currently working on her mother's wartime memoirs.

JAN de GRIJS

Retired. An active member of the Creative Writing Group.

D. SANDY NIELSEN
Retired from 'The Place Where Evil Lurks.' Obsessive-compulsive raconteur. Confessed Vikingophile. Still to be found in the Internet Science Fiction Database at *http://www.isfdb.org/cgi-bin/ea.cgi?121061* with short selection of some previous works. Also involved in other writing groups.

BALA MENON
Journalist-artist-historian-storyteller. Has worked in newspapers in India/Middle East and publishing firms in Toronto. Co-authored a book on the culinary history of the Jews of Cochin in 2013. Now working on two non-fiction, research-based books. Has a popular blog: *http://jewsofcochin.blogspot.ca*

CLIFF TRAVERS
An obvious fan and exponent of the short, short story, Mr. Travers is a man of few words.

EVA BRUNEY
Born on the island of Dominica in the West Indies. Has penned a book of poetry called *"A Little Bit Of Me"*. Mother of two beautiful girls. Has two grandsons and one grand-daughter. Now spends most of her time working on a book of fiction.

BARB McDONALD
An older lady with lots of experience in the ways of the world. Sits and daydreams about days long gone. Now, writing a memoir for family members living in all corners of the world. Her heart still resides in the Jamaican countryside where she spent her childhood.

EILEEN SLEATH
Was for long an active member of the Creative Writing Group, writing stories about her fond memories of family, life in England and in Canada. Works cover many subjects and hopes her grandchildren will enjoy them in the future.

CAROL RAYMOND

Retired teacher; also worked for several years in insurance industry. Currently working on collection of stories for children; also enjoys scrapbooking, geneology, gardening, travel and spending time with grandchildren.

JOY ENGLAND

Leader of Memoirs Writing Group for past 12 years. Past member of Flower City Creative Writing group. Teacher of English language and literature (retired). Enjoys reading, choral singing, yoga and gardening.

DOROTHY COATES

Deceased. Dorothy was a lively and entertaining member of the Creative Writing Group; she would often break into song and brought much life and pleasure to all meetings. Had performed on stage and in a circus in England; she had a marvellous voice and several hearts were broken at the Flower City Recreation Centre when she passed away.